THE EARTH:
Natural Resources and Human Intervention

It would take a planet twice the size of the Earth to provide the entire global population with the same material lifestyle currently enjoyed in the West by 20% of its inhabitants. Even the current consumption of natural resources by the relative few has caused climate change, ever-expanding deserts, dried-up rivers, and erosion on an unprecedented scale. The services of nature – so essential for man's existence and survival – are being damaged daily by the material metabolism of our economy.

For the past 15 years Professor Schmidt-Bleek has demanded a dematerialization of the economy by a factor of 10. Technically this is possible, without reducing the standard of living. But it will only happen if the wrongly set price-signals are adjusted in such a way as to make future-oriented behavior profitable.

Friedrich Schmidt-Bleek is a Professor of Chemistry and taught for many years in the United States of America. Known as the "Father of the German Chemical Law" he was responsible at the OECD for introducing the test methods for chemicals. He was the founding Vice-President of the Wuppertal Institut and was awarded the prestigious World Environment Award in Japan in 2001. Today he heads the Factor 10 Institut in Carnoules (France).

Our addresses on the Internet:
www.the-sustainability-project.com
www.forum-fuer-verantwortung.de
[English version available]

THE EARTH:
Natural Resources and Human Intervention

FRIEDRICH SCHMIDT-BLEEK

Translated by Sandra Lustig

Klaus Wiegandt, General Editor

HAUS PUBLISHING

First published in Great Britain in 2009 by
Haus Publishing Ltd
70 Cadogan Place
London SW1X 9AH
www.hauspublishing.com

Originally published as: FORUM FÜR VERANTWORTUNG *Nutzen wir die Erde richtig? Die Leistungen der Natur und die Arbeit des Menschen*, by Friedrich Schmidt-Bleek. Ed. by Klaus Wiegandt

© 2007 Fischer Taschenbuch Verlag in der S. Fischer Verlag GmbH, Frankfurt am Main

English translation copyright © Sandra Lustig 2008

The moral right of the author has been asserted

A CIP catalogue record for this book
is available from the British Library

ISBN 978-1-906598-09-9

Typeset in Sabon by MacGuru Ltd
Printed in Dubai by Oriental Press

Mixed Sources
Product group from well-managed forests and other controlled sources
www.fsc.org Cert no. CU-COC-809367
© 1996 Forest Stewardship Council

Haus Publishing believes in the importance of a sustainable future for our planet. This book is printed on paper produced in accordance with the standards of sustainability set out and monitored by the FSC. The printer holds chain of custody.

Contents

Sales of the German-language edition of this series have exceeded all expectations. The positive media response has been encouraging, too. Both of these positive responses demonstrate that the series addresses the right topics in a language that is easily understood by the general reader. The combination of thematic breadth and scientifically astute, yet generally accessible writing, is particularly important as I believe it to be a vital prerequisite for smoothing the way to a sustainable society by turning knowledge into action. After all, I am not a scientist myself; my background is in business.

A few months ago, shortly after the first volumes had been published, we received suggestions from neighboring countries in Europe recommending that an English-language edition would reach a far larger readership. Books dealing with global challenges, they said, require global action brought about by informed debate amongst as large an audience as possible. When delegates from India, China, and Pakistan voiced similar concerns at an international conference my mind was made up. Dedicated individuals such as Lester R. Brown and Jonathan Porritt deserve credit for bringing the concept of sustainability to the attention of the general public, I am convinced that this series can give the discourse about sustainability something new.

Two years have passed since I wrote the foreword to the initial German edition. During this time, unsustainable developments on our planet have come to our attention in ever more dramatic ways. The price of oil has nearly tripled; the value of industrial metals has risen exponentially and, quite unexpectedly, the costs of staple foods such as corn, rice, and wheat have reached all-time highs. Around the globe, people are increasingly concerned that the pressure caused by these drastic price increases will lead to serious destabilization in China, India, Indonesia, Vietnam, and Malaysia, the world's key developing regions.

The frequency and intensity of natural disasters brought on by global warming has continued to increase. Many regions of our Earth are experiencing prolonged droughts, with subsequent shortages of drinking water and the destruction of entire harvests. In other parts of the world, typhoons and hurricanes are causing massive flooding and inflicting immeasurable suffering.

The turbulence in the world's financial markets, triggered by the US sub-prime mortgage crisis, has only added to these woes. It has affected every country and made clear just how unscrupulous and sometimes irresponsible speculation has become in today's financial world. The expectation of exorbitant short-term rates of return on capital investments led to complex and obscure financial engineering. Coupled with a reckless willingness to take risks everyone involved seemingly lost track of the situation. How else can blue chip companies incur multi-billion dollar losses? If central banks had not come to the rescue with dramatic steps to back up their currencies, the world's economy would have collapsed. It was only in these circumstances that the use of public monies could be justified. It is therefore imperative to prevent a repeat of speculation with short-term capital on such a gigantic scale.

Taken together, these developments have at least significantly improved the readiness for a debate on sustainability. Many more are now aware that our wasteful use of natural resources and energy have serious consequences, and not only for future generations.

Two years ago, who would have dared to hope that WalMart, the world's largest retailer, would initiate a dialog about sustainability with its customers and promise to put the results into practice? Who would have considered it possible that CNN would start a series "Going Green?" Every day, more and more businesses worldwide announce that they are putting the topic of sustainability at the core of their strategic considerations. Let us use this momentum to try and make sure that these positive developments are not a flash in the pan, but a solid part of our necessary discourse within civic society.

However, we cannot achieve sustainable development through a multitude of individual adjustments. We are facing the challenge of critical fundamental questioning of our lifestyle and consumption and patterns of production. We must grapple with the complexity of the entire earth system in a forward-looking and precautionary manner, and not focus solely on topics such as energy and climate change.

The authors of these twelve books examine the consequences of our destructive interference in the Earth ecosystem from different perspectives. They point out that we still have plenty of opportunities to shape a sustainable future. If we want to achieve this, however, it is imperative that we use the information we have as a basis for systematic action, guided by the principles of sustainable development. If the step from knowledge to action is not only to be taken, but also to succeed, we need to offer comprehensive education to all, with the foundation in early childhood. The central issues of the future must be anchored firmly in school curricula, and no university student should be permitted to graduate without having completed a general course on sustainable development. Everyday opportunities for action must be made clear to us all – young and old. Only then can we begin to think critically about our lifestyles and make positive changes in the direction of sustainability. We need to show the business community the way to sustainable development via a responsible attitude to consumption, and become active within our sphere of influence as opinion leaders.

For this reason, my foundation *Forum für Verantwortung*, the ASKO EUROPA-FOUNDATION, and the European Academy Otzenhausen have joined forces to produce educational materials on the future of the Earth to accompany the twelve books developed at the renowned Wuppertal Institute for Climate, Environment and Energy. We are setting up an extensive program of seminars, and the initial results are very promising. The success of our initiative "Encouraging Sustainability," which has now been awarded the status of an official project of the UN Decade "Education for Sustainable Development," confirms the public's great interest in, and demand for, well-founded information.

I would like to thank the authors for their additional effort to update all their information and put the contents of their original volumes in a more global context. My special thanks goes to the translators, who submitted themselves to a strict timetable, and to Annette Maas for coordinating the Sustainability Project. I am grateful for the expert editorial advice of Amy Irvine and the Haus Publishing editorial team for not losing track of the "3600-page-work."

Taking action – out of insight and responsibility

"We were on our way to becoming gods, supreme beings who could create a second world, using the natural world only as building blocks for our new creation."

This warning by the psychoanalyst and social philosopher Erich Fromm is to be found in *To Have or to Be?* (1976). It aptly expresses the dilemma in which we find ourselves as a result of our scientific-technical orientation.

The original intention of submitting to nature in order to make use of it ("knowledge is power") evolved into subjugating nature in order to exploit it. We have left the earlier successful path with its many advances and are now on the wrong track, a path of danger with incalculable risks. The greatest danger stems from the unshakable faith of the overwhelming majority of politicians and business leaders in unlimited economic growth which, together with limitless technological innovation, is supposed to provide solutions to all the challenges of the present and the future.

For decades now, scientists have been warning of this collision course with nature. As early as 1983, the United Nations founded the World Commission on Environment and Development which published the Brundtland Report in 1987. Under the title *Our Common Future*, it presented a concept that could save mankind from catastrophe and help to find the way back to a responsible way of life, the concept of long-term environmentally sustainable use of resources. "Sustainability," as used in the Brundtland Report, means "development that meets the needs of the present without compromising the ability of future generations to meet their own needs."

Despite many efforts, this guiding principle for ecologically, economically, and socially sustainable action has unfortunately not yet become the reality it can, indeed must, become. I believe the reason for this is that civil societies have not yet been sufficiently informed and mobilized.

Forum für Verantwortung

Against this background, and in the light of ever more warnings and scientific results, I decided to take on a societal responsibility with my foundation. I would like to contribute to the expansion of public discourse about sustainable development which is absolutely essential. It is my desire to provide a large number of people with facts and contextual knowledge on the subject of sustainability, and to show alternative options for future action.

After all, the principle of "sustainable development" alone is insufficient to change current patterns of living and economic practices. It does provide some orientation, but it has to be negotiated in concrete terms within society and then implemented in patterns of behavior. A democratic society seriously seeking to reorient itself towards future viability must rely on critical, creative individuals capable of both discussion and action. For this reason, life-long learning, from childhood to old age, is a necessary precondition for realizing sustainable development. The practical implementation of the ecological, economic, and social goals of a sustainability strategy in economic policy requires people able to reflect, innovate and recognize potentials for structural change and learn to use them in the best interests of society.

It is not enough for individuals to be merely "concerned." On the contrary, it is necessary to understand the scientific background and interconnections in order to have access to them and be able to develop them in discussions that lead in the right direction. Only in this way can the ability to make appropriate judgments emerge, and this is a prerequisite for responsible action.

The essential condition for this is presentation of both the facts and the theories within whose framework possible courses of action are visible in a manner that is both appropriate to the subject matter and comprehensible. Then, people will be able to use them to guide their personal behavior.

In order to move towards this goal, I asked renowned scientists to present in a generally understandable way the state of research and the possible options on twelve important topics in the area of sustainable development in the series "*Forum für Verantwortung.*" All those involved in this project are in agreement that there is no alternative to a united path of all societies towards sustainability:

- *Our Planet: How Much More Can Earth Take?* (Jill Jäger)
- *Energy: The World's Race for Resources in the 21st Century* (Hermann-Joseph Wagner)
- *Our Threatened Oceans* (Stefan Rahmstorf and Katherine Richardson)
- *Water Resources: Efficient, Sustainable and Equitable Use* (Wolfram Mauser)
- *The Earth: Natural Resources and Human Intervention* (Friedrich Schmidt-Bleek)
- *Overcrowded World? Global Population and International Migration* (Rainer Münz and Albert F. Reiterer)
- *Feeding the Planet: Environmental Protection through Sustainable Agriculture* (Klaus Hahlbrock)
- *Costing the Earth? Perspectives on Sustainable Development* (Bernd Meyer)

The public debate

What gives me the courage to carry out this project and the optimism that I will reach civil societies in this way, and possibly provide an impetus for change?

For one thing, I have observed that, because of the number and severity of natural disasters in recent years, people have become more sensitive concerning questions of how we treat the Earth. For another, there are scarcely any books on the market that cover in language comprehensible to civil society the broad spectrum of comprehensive sustainable development in an integrated manner.

When I began to structure my ideas and the prerequisites for a public discourse on sustainability in 2004, I could not foresee that by the time the first books of the series were published, the general public would have come to perceive at least climate change and energy as topics of great concern. I believe this occurred especially as a result of the following events:

First, the United States witnessed the devastation of New Orleans in August 2005 by Hurricane Katrina, and the anarchy following in the wake of this disaster.

Second, in 2006, Al Gore began his information campaign on climate change and wastage of energy, culminating in his film *An*

Inconvenient Truth, which has made an impression on a wide audience of all age groups around the world.

Third, the 700-page Stern Report, commissioned by the British government, published in 2007 by the former Chief Economist of the World Bank Nicholas Stern in collaboration with other economists, was a wake-up call for politicians and business leaders alike. This report makes clear how extensive the damage to the global economy will be if we continue with "business as usual" and do not take vigorous steps to halt climate change. At the same time, the report demonstrates that we could finance countermeasures for just one-tenth of the cost of the probable damage, and could limit average global warming to 2° C – if we only took action.

Fourth, the most recent IPCC report, published in early 2007, was met by especially intense media interest, and therefore also received considerable public attention. It laid bare as never before how serious the situation is, and called for drastic action against climate change.

Last, but not least, the exceptional commitment of a number of billionaires such as Bill Gates, Warren Buffett, George Soros, and Richard Branson as well as Bill Clinton's work to "save the world" is impressing people around the globe and deserves mention here.

An important task for the authors of our twelve-volume series was to provide appropriate steps towards sustainable development in their particular subject area. In this context, we must always be aware that successful transition to this type of economic, ecological, and social development on our planet cannot succeed immediately, but will require many decades. Today, there are still no sure formulae for the most successful long-term path. A large number of scientists and even more innovative entrepreneurs and managers will have to use their creativity and dynamism to solve the great challenges. Nonetheless, even today, we can discern the first clear goals we must reach in order to avert a looming catastrophe. And billions of consumers around the world can use their daily purchasing decisions to help both ease and significantly accelerate the economy's transition to sustainable development – provided the political framework is there. In addition, from a global perspective, billions of citizens have the opportunity to mark out the political "guide rails" in a democratic way via their parliaments.

The most important insight currently shared by the scientific, political, and economic communities is that our resource-intensive Western model of prosperity (enjoyed today by one billion people) cannot be extended to another five billion or, by 2050, at least eight billion people. That would go far beyond the biophysical capacity of the planet. This realization is not in dispute. At issue, however, are the consequences we need to draw from it.

If we want to avoid serious conflicts between nations, the industrialized countries must reduce their consumption of resources by more than the developing and threshold countries increase theirs. In the future, all countries must achieve the same level of consumption. Only then will we be able to create the necessary ecological room for maneuver in order to ensure an appropriate level of prosperity for developing and threshold countries.

To avoid a dramatic loss of prosperity in the West during this long-term process of adaptation, the transition from high to low resource use, that is, to an ecological market economy, must be set in motion quickly.

On the other hand, the threshold and developing countries must commit themselves to getting their population growth under control within the foreseeable future. The twenty-year Programme of Action adopted by the United Nations International Conference on Population and Development in Cairo in 1994 must be implemented with stronger support from the industrialized nations.

If humankind does not succeed in drastically improving resource and energy efficiency and reducing population growth in a sustainable manner – we should remind ourselves of the United Nations forecast that population growth will come to a halt only at the end of this century, with a world population of eleven to twelve billion – then we run the real risk of developing eco-dictatorships. In the words of Ernst Ulrich von Weizsäcker: "States will be sorely tempted to ration limited resources, to micromanage economic activity, and in the interest of the environment to specify from above what citizens may or may not do. 'Quality-of-life' experts might define in an authoritarian way what kind of needs people are permitted to satisfy." (*Earth Politics*, 1989, in English translation: 1994).

It is time

It is time for us to take stock in a fundamental and critical way. We, the public, must decide what kind of future we want. Progress and quality of life is not dependent on year-by-year growth in per capita income alone, nor do we need inexorably growing amounts of goods to satisfy our needs. The short-term goals of our economy, such as maximizing profits and accumulating capital, are major obstacles to sustainable development. We should go back to a more decentralized economy and reduce world trade and the waste of energy associated with it in a targeted fashion. If resources and energy were to cost their "true" prices, the global process of rationalization and labor displacement will be reversed, because cost pressure will be shifted to the areas of materials and energy.

The path to sustainability requires enormous technological innovations. But not everything that is technologically possible has to be put into practice. We should not strive to place all areas of our lives under the dictates of the economic system. Making justice and fairness a reality for everyone is not only a moral and ethical imperative, but is also the most important means of securing world peace in the long term. For this reason, it is essential to place the political relationship between states and peoples on a new basis, a basis with which everyone can identify, not only the most powerful. Without common principles of global governance, sustainability cannot become a reality in any of the fields discussed in this series.

And finally, we must ask whether we humans have the right to reproduce to such an extent that we may reach a population of eleven to twelve billion by the end of this century, laying claim to every square centimeter of our Earth and restricting and destroying the habitats and way of life of all other species to an ever greater degree.

Our future is not predetermined. We ourselves shape it by our actions. We can continue as before, but if we do so, we will put ourselves in the biophysical straitjacket of nature, with possibly disastrous political implications, by the middle of this century. But we also have the opportunity to create a fairer and more viable future for ourselves and for future generations. This requires the commitment of everyone on our planet.

Klaus Wiegandt

Summer 2008

Preface

How environmental protection mutated into an eco-strategy

It was December 31, 1988. We were having a New Year's Party with some Russian friends near Vienna, in a snowy village by the name of Biedermannsdorf, to be precise. One of our guests was Stash Shatalin, at the time President Gorbachev's chief economic advisor. He had brought some vodka, and Marie had prepared a French meal with wine from Provence. As the evening drew on and some of our guests struck up songs in honor of Mother Russia, I turned to Stash with a question that had concerned me for quite some time. I wanted to know whether the time had come to establish the successful Western model of environmental protection in the Soviet Union as well. After all, at the request of the Kremlin, we had discussed a number of draft laws for Russia's economic future and adapted them to Western conceptions at IIASA (International Institute for Applied Systems Analysis in Laxenburg near Vienna). In the process, we had learned about the poor condition of the environment in the Soviet Union, and it seemed to me that it was time to begin to protect the environment as we had done in the West. The response to my question was cool, crisp, and clear: "Nyet." And the explanation brought me back down to earth with a thud. For Stash Shatalin spelled out his answer with the words, "Only when we have become as rich as you have in the

West with a market economy will we be able to pay for your kind of environmental protection."

That hit home. Apparently, something had gone terribly wrong with old-style environmental protection. It seemed that we had developed measures to protect planet Earth that only the rich countries could afford. If not even Russia was in a position to afford this Western-style environmental protection, what about many other countries? How were China, India, Indonesia, and Brazil, for example, to solve their environmental problems? And what would happen if the prosperous OECD (Organisation for Economic Co-operation and Development) countries were at some point to hit hard times?

I could not stop thinking about the question as to where the mistake in our thinking and our system might be. If it was all we could do to carry out environmental protection in one or two dozen countries with costly, government-regulated measures, then saving planet Earth would be well-nigh impossible. And even if we waited for decades for the other countries to become rich – wasn't creating our lifestyle itself the deeper reason for the progressing plight of the environment? It was remarkable: none other than an economist originally dedicated to the Russian planned economy put his finger on the flaw of our Western system: it is systematically impossible to remedy fundamental failings of the economy by means of individual reactive measures. This I now understood. But how could we move forward?

The previous year, sustainability of human society had been proclaimed as the uppermost global goal. From then on, the world economy was to create prosperity for all in a socially just way and at peace with the ecosphere! As clear as that sounds, it was also clear that rarely in the history of humankind had a goal had so little to do with reality!

The big question is: how can we live in such a way that life will also be possible in the future? In other words, the issue is sustainability, future viability, and one can define this concept as the capability of the economy to create prosperity for all and simultaneously to secure, at the global level, the natural, social, and economic foundations on which this capability depends for the future.

After the conversation with Stash Shatalin, I began to ferret out the roots of our problems with the environment. For what reason was our pattern of prosperity incompatible with the preservation of a healthy environment? By which means and how are we changing the natural biogeochemical cycles? Why do we have to fear that we are damaging the priceless services of nature without which we would never have come into being and which we need in order to survive?

These services include, for example, availability of healthy water, pure air for breathing, the formation and preservation of fertile soils, protection from dangerous radiation from outer space, diversity of species, and the capability of sperm to procreate. If these services of the ecosphere were traded on the market, they would obviously be infinitely expensive. And even if one were inclined to spend a lot of money on them, it would all remain limited to small areas and would not be replaceable by technology for a long time to come.

While I was pondering this insight, a new idea came to me in a flash, which in retrospect seems trivial. I became aware of the following: the more natural resources we pump through our economy, the more of our raw materials we use up to technically create each and every bit of utility, the more we change the basis available to support our life on Earth. For every time we move mass by technical means, every time we extract resources from nature, it changes the web of its dynamic equilibriums, thereby influencing the continuing evolution of the ecosphere with an uncertain outcome.

And this idea goes further: for the resource flows caused by technology are not only changing the dynamics of ecological equilibriums, they are also denaturing ever greater parts of the Earth's surface. Of course, nature reacts to all these billions of man-made changes. It creates new equilibriums, it adapts to the new situation. In short, it is in a process of transformation. No science and no computer program will ever be able to predict, recognize, and explain the diversity and intensity of these changes, let alone undo them.

The conclusion from my insight was as trivial as the insight itself: the better the material efficiency, the less surface area is sealed, in other words, the higher the resource productivity of all processes, goods, and services becomes, the less we will overstrain the ecosphere that supports us. To use an image: we should organize the economy within the well-defined corridors determined by nature. This means that preventive environmental protection and sustainable economic policy require above all that we use natural resources much more sparingly than we have become accustomed to doing in the frenzy of growth during the last century.

Just before the end of her career as the German Federal Minister of the Environment in 1998, Angela Merkel effected a cabinet decision with the goal of increasing the resource productivity of the German economy by a factor of 2.5 by the year 2005. After the Green Party took over government responsibility for protecting the ecosphere, they did not pursue this idea further. Resource productivity plays a still somewhat cautious, but highly visible new role as a strategic element in the coalition agreement of November 2005. On January 9, 2006, the German Federal Minister of the Environment, Sigmar Gabriel told the *Süddeutsche Zeitung* (a major daily newspaper), "There are many indications that energy and resource intelligence will become the fundamental technology of our century."

We must succeed in pursuing holistic policies to create sustainable prosperity. We cannot yet discern how the different dimensions of sustainability can be joined with one another to lead to balanced political decisions. This book seeks to give you an understanding of what we as citizens can do to contribute to shaping the future in Europe. Promoting welfare will play a central role.

Acknowledgments

Many thanks to Klaus Wiegandt for his foresight and his untiring support for making the "Forum for Responsibility" series become reality. May these volumes contribute to paving the way – which is becoming ever more difficult – towards economic, social, and ecological sustainability of our existence on this planet.

It is a particular pleasure to thank Ernst Peter Fischer for his help. It is he who enriched my vision and my ideas and helped me clarify them so I could present them to the readers of this book. Willy Bierter undertook the task of smoothing out imperfections in the text in the final stages, and I would like to express my gratitude for that as well.

Once again, I would like to use this opportunity to thank my former staff in Wuppertal for their efforts to make our concepts "Factor 10" and "MIPS" recognized and effective. In particular, these thanks are due Stefan Bringezu, Friedrich Hinterberger, Christa Liedtke, Christopher Manstein, Joachim Spangenberg, Hartmut Stiller, and Jolla Welfens. Thanks also to Harry Lehman for his knowledge and astute criticism which accompanied me from the beginning.

I would like to call out my thanks to my friends around the world for disseminating and deepening "Factor 10."

Without Marie's patience of a saint, this book would never have seen the light of day. Thank you forever – and much more than mere thanks.

This book is dedicated to our seven children and their partners, and especially to their seventeen children.

Carnoules/Provence, May, 2006

1 The Earth In Motion

People work to make a better world, and they want to use nature to this end. They invented science in order to do so as efficiently and as successfully as possible. Knowledge of the laws of nature puts us in a position to use them "to ease human existence," as Bertolt Brecht had his protagonist Galilei say. And it need not be emphasized that in doing so, many people were able to achieve appreciable prosperity with comprehensive material and social security in the past centuries – first in Europe, and then also in other parts of the world.

But our use of nature extends beyond applying its laws. We tend to use nature even more by consuming the resources it supplies us free of charge, for example in the form of oil, minerals, land, and water. And we expend immense amounts of energy to transform these resources into gigantic materials flows which circle the globe to reach the places where the people live who would like their needs to be satisfied. For quite some time, we have increasingly been setting the Earth in motion to promote our welfare, and we have been realizing much too slowly and only bit by bit that this *modus operandi* has limits. Many scientists who study questions relating to economic and ecological systems agree that there are not even close to enough raw materials available on our planet, were everyone to consume as much of them as the current top consumers in Europe and America.

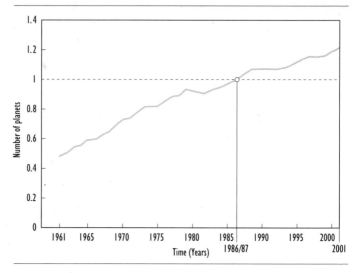

Figure 1   Consumption of a planet

Every country needs land to produce food for its population, have access to
water, build housing and infrastructure, provide jobs and security as well as
create recreational areas. The "Ecological Footprint" developed by Mathis
Wackernagel is a metric for this concept. It indicates that year by year, the
world is consuming more resources than nature can renew. And the portion we
use in the West is about 80% of the total. In other words, we are consuming
significantly more than our fair share, while mankind is growing by 80 million
people per year!

How we manage natural resources

One consequence resulting from this state of affairs is our society's obligation to attain a symbiosis between environmental
protection and a market economy. In other words, we should
attempt to make more out of the resources we take from the
environment than we have to date. If we were to use products
and environmental goods (water, mineral resources, soils, etc.)
more efficiently, then we would not only need to extract a smaller

Environmental indicator	Trend
Atmosphere	The global climate has warmed by 0.6 to 0.7 °C in the last 100 years; most of global warming is due to human activities.
Wetlands	Since 1900, more than half of global wetlands which contribute to the hydrologic cycle and to biological diversity have been lost.
Biological diversity	Both in the oceans and on land, loss of species has increased sharply; it has been said that the Earth is currently in the sixth period of extinction in its history.
Soil and land	An estimated 50% of the global land area has been impacted due to direct human influence; the quality of 23% of the usable land area has worsened with consequences for productivity.
Water	More than half of the accessible freshwater is used for human purposes, resulting in the mining and overuse of gigantic subterranean freshwater sources.
Forests	Forest areas have been diminished from 6 to 3.9 billion hectares over the course of human history; in twenty-nine countries, more than 90% of the forest has been lost since the 16th century; in the 1990s, global forest areas were reduced by 4.2%.
Fishing grounds	The overuse of numerous fish stocks is putting the ecological balance of the oceans and coastal ecosystems at risk; according to the FAO, more than one-quarter of all fish stocks are currently depleted or threatened by depletion; and a further 50% are being fished at the biological limit.

Table 1 Some global trends of resource consumption

amount of resources from nature. We would also have an easier time dealing with a problem which, historically speaking, has been a decisive challenge for environmental protection: namely waste which we introduce into the environment and which

---

Natural resources

Natural resources are all naturally available abiotic and biotic raw materials (minerals, fossil and nuclear energy carriers, plants, wild animals, and biodiversity), flow resources (wind, geothermal, tidal, and solar energy), air, water, soil, and space (land use for human settlements, infrastructures, industry, mineral extraction, agriculture, and forestry).

---

becomes a burden for the soil, the air, and the water. For if we could succeed in creating prosperity comparable to the level we have today with lower resource use – if, in other words, it were possible to enhance resource productivity in a targeted and planned fashion – then, in the end, our economy would produce fewer emissions and wastes, including not only products at the end of their lifespan, but also demolished buildings and infrastructure facilities such as roads, bridges, and the like. Resources cost money, so, under favorable circumstances, a two-fold profit could emerge if we manage them appropriately, namely lower costs for our material prosperity and simultaneously less stress on the ecosphere.

We must dampen our economy's hunger for ever greater amounts of raw materials. One of the great tasks for the future lies in dematerializing the economy and finding other ways of developing and paths for growth.

Dematerialization of the economy

The presidents and heads of government of the EU member states recognized as early as 2001 that, as we are urgently recommending here, we must "decouple economic growth from resource use." This is a precondition if we are to reach the goal which by now has become a household word: "sustainable development." Development is considered sustainable if it takes the limited amounts of natural resources into consideration and is designed to avoid all tendencies which could place restrictions on the quality of life of future generations.

Sustainable development means an improvement of living conditions, more contentment and well-being, in safety and dignity for the large majority of human beings alive today. And that is what this book is about. It does not preach limiting the level of prosperity we have attained, but seeks to point out pathways towards the successful achievement of sustainable growth even at the global level by cutting back resource use in a targeted fashion, which would also enable such growth to benefit a larger number of people.

We mentioned the concept of dematerialization as a key word. Once this goal has been understood and accepted, technical and economic imagination will use it as a point of orientation, in contrast to the goals of the past. An entirely new market for eco-intelligent products and services could emerge, as we will elaborate below. The potential for innovation would be enormous, and it would provide opportunities for alert entrepreneurs and businesspeople to earn additional profits, employing greater decision-making skills and better ideas than the competition. At the same time, new jobs could be created. These challenges and the favorable opportunities for the economy are a central theme of this book.

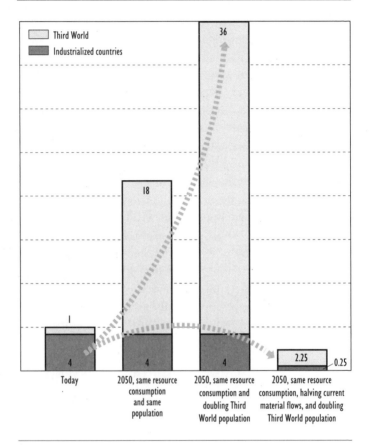

Figure 2 Access to global material flows provides the foundation for material prosperity

Calculated per capita, it is distributed very unevenly today. If the number of people in the "Third World" continues to increase, and if their consumption approaches that of the industrialized countries, we would need seven times the amount of resources in 2050 that we do today. Our ecosphere, already overextended today, would not be able to provide the necessary resources. In order to secure its vital services, we must reduce material flows, that is, we must dematerialize the economy.

Moving resources

I first put forward my vision of a dematerialized economy in book form in 1993. To my own surprise, I had realized that in the environmental protection practices of the day, we had almost completely overlooked something, namely the immense movements of material for which we are responsible! Even when we merely remove raw materials from their natural locations in their deposits on our planet, even if we just transport them to another location, it disrupts the ecosphere and its evolution substantially, even if we do not use the masses we have moved to enhance our prosperity at all.

To give an example for this type of development, I would like to remind the reader that the waste material from mining – for instance in the strip mines near Jülich, west of Cologne, Germany – is not a problem of hazardous substances, not a problem of biodegradability, and not a problem of waste disposal. These mountains of overburden do not contribute to the profits of those responsible for creating them, either. On the contrary, they cost a lot of money. They are not the subject of classical environmental policy. But certainly nobody will doubt that the heaps of mining waste could be anything but a consequence of a dramatic intrusion in nature and stand before us as products of a material-intensive economy.

One more example from mining to call our attention to the consequences of man-made material flows: the subterranean shafts out of which the coal in Germany's Ruhr district was dug are collapsing today. The earth has sunk by about six meters on an area of 70,000 hectares. What is the consequence?

If enormous amounts of water were not pumped out day and night, huge lakes would have formed where several million people live today, and where thousands of businesses provide

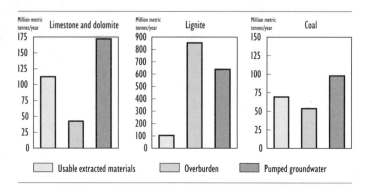

Figure 3   Comparison of different ecological rucksacks (overburden and
            water) for resource extraction in the former West Germany,
            1990

jobs. At some point in the not-too-distant future, the energy
employed for pumping the water will surpass the energy derived
from the coal. For many years to come, future generations will
have to continue paying the bill for the 20th century's hunger for
technology without benefiting from it.

One day, plants will spring up on the mining waste heaps, of
course. There are even plans for sledding near Jülich. Nature can
"repair" a lot, and sometimes even more than pessimists give
it credit for. But it needs time to do so. If mankind's interferences in the ecosphere upset nature so quickly that natural processes can no longer take hold, then the threshold of overuse will
increasingly be overstepped. In this case, we are leading a life
which will be possible in this form only for a limited period of
time – just for so long until we have used up or carried away and
destroyed the resources our planet has to offer. This would mean
that our lifestyle and our economy would not be sustainable, and
it is urgent that we draw the consequences from this insight.

Moving materials on this planet by technical means and the seemingly boundless possibilities for generating energy and using other resources which we imagine to be available eternally have been major obstacles to establishing our economic system in such a way that human life on this planet can become sustainable. We should not lose sight of the fact that the human economy is akin to a parasite that is dependent upon its ecosphere. Our life is possible only with the ecosphere, and if we do not make any changes, we will be well on the way towards jeopardizing our own survival by thoughtlessly and negligently placing excessive demands on our host, Earth.

From an ecological point of view, however, the most urgent task is not to decrease the burden on individual resources and preserve them for future generations, as many, including well-known scientists, have been calling upon us to do since the 1970s. From today's perspective, the goal must rather be that resources are to be extracted from nature, moved, and transformed in a measured way. The material flows and their ecological consequences are the acute problem, not the amount of resources future generations will find available for their purposes in their natural locations in and on Earth.

In the last forty years, almost one-third of the world's arable land has been lost to erosion (cf. Table 1). And this happened mainly because we talked ourselves into believing that agriculture is an industry like any other, an industry that lives on producing more and more food with bigger and bigger machines and less and less manpower. Statisticians like to use such figures to prove our superiority over people who still take the preservation of topsoil seriously. Approximately ten million hectares of farmland are lost every year, 75 billion metric tons of soil.

It is frightening to see the fatalism with which this ecological catastrophe is tolerated – at least seemingly – around the world, in contrast to, for example, the dangers posed by terrorists. Apparently, many people cannot imagine a form of agriculture that meets their enormous need for food, and in such a way that it can perform to this standard tomorrow, in twenty years, and even in a hundred. Yet this is exactly what our goal must be if we want there to be a future for billions of people on our limited planet, with their wealth of different cultures.

Politically speaking, the perspective of being able to reduce the waste flows and emissions of the economy decisively by means of dematerialization ought to be highly welcome. We should be aware that guiding today's torrents of materials in a "closed-loop economy" would not really mitigate negative impacts. Every loop needs energy and additional machines; it requires transportation, thus spawning additional material flows. And what is more, chemical and technical cycles are never able to recover 100% of the materials used initially. After aluminum, for instance, is recycled fifteen times, less than 3% of the metal is left. This makes it unavoidable to refill the economy with fresh natural resources, especially in light of the fact that substantially less than 100% of the "old" aluminum can be collected.

All the enthusiasm for closing loops and recycling makes it easy to forget that it is not possible to technically recycle more than 30% of the mass moved today, as we will show below. The necessary easing of the burden on the environment will be possible only if we avoid the tremendous resource flows in our economy *a priori* – and the challenge is to learn how to do so.

A metric I introduced (MIPS), and which will be explained below, helps us to calculate for every individual case whether and to what extent recycling is worthwhile, from the perspective of resource productivity. For example, the business Hans Sperger in Vorarlberg, Austria (www.putzlappen.at) markets both single-use and multi-use rags for cleaning. The rags are made from old clothes. The single-use rags, including environmentally-sound waste disposal, are approximately 40% cheaper, and their resource productivity is superior to that of the multi-use system by a factor of eight (that is, 800%).

It is a truism to say that if you put a lot into an economy at the front end, you can't prevent a lot from coming out again at the back. This refers to resource flows such as energy carriers, ores, sand, and water that are put into producing, transporting, using, preserving, recycling, and disposing of products, buildings, and infrastructures in order to secure the level of material prosperity we are used to, and to enhance it.

But it is also true that two generations since World War II have become accustomed to the erroneous belief that there are no limits to growth; growth which is still considered the utmost goal, which many still swear by (and which is, in Germany, pre-scribed by law). And we have become more demanding. While in 1950, our grandmothers dreamed of running hot water, many people today believe that owning a car and a lot of other technical equipment that uses energy is a basic human right.

Changing the way we manage the economy

Since the United Nations Conference on Environment and Development (UNCED) in Rio de Janeiro in 1992 at the latest, people around the world have become aware that creating a sustainable economy under stable ecological framework conditions is a significant global issue.

In order to reach this goal, we must shift our attention toward something new. For as long as environmental policy concentrates on the back end of the economy – on avoiding emissions and on the reuse and disposal of waste – and as long as the quality of techniques which have functioned traditionally is not fundamentally thrown into question, environmental protection engenders additional costs for everything it does, and sustainability, the ultimate goal, recedes into the distance. A sustainable economy must remain a distant utopian dream because it has proved unrealistic to trace all known environmental damage back to just one single relevant cause, namely that our economy emits too many "damaging waste materials" to the soil, the air, and the water.

Aside from the fact that the constant and never-ending cleanup at the back end of the economy engenders more and more costs, it also completely fails to address a decisive share of the environmental problems. These environmental problems arise simply from the fact that moving material from its natural deposits causes disturbances of ecological developments – regardless of whether we produce goods for our prosperous lifestyle or simply pile them up as mining waste heaps. As already indicated above: the most important ecological problem is the material flows which we set in motion on this planet using technical means (Fig. 4). These material flows, however, originate at the front end of our economy, not at the back. To date, our focus has been one-sided, concentrating on what comes out of the machinery that generates prosperity and consumption. Now it is time to turn our attention to what is introduced into this machinery at the beginning. That is what this book is about.

When "economic life" still meant that several million people around the world dug holes with their hands, cultivated fields with oxen, built protective ramparts, discovered water power, and used wind to make flour out of grain, the Earth could often still cope with these man-made interferences; admittedly, its naturally occurring dynamics of change were disturbed, but this had no consequences at the particular time. In North Africa and the former Yugoslavia, for example, traces of man-made devastation

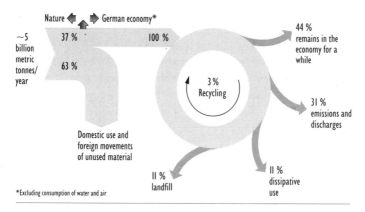

Figure 4 Material flows in billions of metric tons per year, caused by creating material prosperity in Germany (former West German states) in the year 2000, excluding consumption of water and air

The significant end points, after passage through the economy, are given in percent. The figure shows that approximately two-thirds of the amount of natural materials originally set in motion do not even enter the prosperity machine. This refers, for example, to overburden from mining operations and the unusable amounts of tailings that accrue when ore is mined. A significant portion of them remains in other countries, but must be included when calculating the ecological rucksacks of imports to Germany. (The figures were kindly provided by H. Schütz of the Wuppertal Institute.)

dating from long before industrialization can be found to this day. When Rome still dominated the Mediterranean region, it used up the fertility of North African topsoil to produce bread for its marauding bands of soldiers. We now find desert there. And Venice cut down the woods of western Yugoslavia to build its merchant fleets. Today, only karst is left.

Since the technical genius James Watt developed his steam engine and paved the way for penetrating the entrails of the Earth with the growing power of machinery, a fundamental change in the relationship between man and the ecosphere has taken place.

Hardly a square kilometer of the Earth's surface remains which is not cultivated or changed indirectly by technical means.

We humans are changing this Earth dramatically and on a large scale, and all too often, we do not even know what we are doing. Our species is employing modern technology to influence our ecological surroundings in four ways:

1. Mankind is moving and extracting ever greater amounts of solid substances and water from the Earth: to generate energy, to produce goods, to construct infrastructures and buildings, water for drinking, cleaning, and cooling in private homes and in industry, to irrigate fields, and to generate hydropower. The amounts we actually use constitute only a fraction of the mountains of materials moved, and of the mountains of substances left behind, for example as mining waste with no market value at all.

   The amount of mass moved on the continents by modern technology is several times as great as the amount moved naturally by geological forces. Natural forces such as wind and water are no longer predominant when it comes to shaping the planet; mankind has surpassed them with technical means. In the United States, it is estimated that almost eight times as much is moved by artificial means as by natural ones.

   In the process, substances are emitted which contaminate air, soils, and waterways. They include toxics, for instance asbestos dust, cyanides from gold mining, sedimentation of cadmium and other heavy metals in rivers, and wastewater from coal mining that is as acidic as sulfuric acid.

2. Day by day, mankind is using more of our planet's land area for agriculture, building roads and industrial facilities, and constructing residential buildings.

3. All the raw materials used by industry are denatured by man in order to generate material prosperity. Their physical and chemical characteristics are changed employing energy. In doing so, poisons are produced intentionally, for example chemicals for agriculture, organic solvents such as acetone, for instance as nail polish remover, or materials which can have poisonous properties under certain conditions, such as medicines.

4. We return most of what we remove from the environment back to it in the form of waste within a short time. With the exception of old structures such as the pyramids in Egypt, wats in Asia, ramparts, and cathedrals, little that mankind has created has remained for long periods of time.

In Germany alone, seventy metric tons of nature – not counting water and air – is consumed per person per year, and only approximately 20% of that amount remains in our technosphere (the part of the ecosphere that encompasses all things produced and changed by mankind) for more than a year. More than 50% of the materials used technically in Germany are imported from different countries.

When waste reverts back to "Mother Nature's cradle," it again causes changes in the ecosphere whose nature and magnitude we know little about.

Our knowledge about large-scale and global consequences is limited in most cases to the knowledge gained by limited local analyses. We also rarely know much about the speed at which the changes we trigger take place. Often, we determine much too late how massive the effects of our actions are. In addition, many changes occur so slowly that a human life is not long enough to notice them. Changes of this nature can frequently be measured only with scientific methods. But what is so slow

that man cannot perceive it may be so fast that the ecosphere
cannot adapt.

The necessity of dematerialization

In 1990, every German "consumed" approximately seventy
metric tons of solid materials from the environment as well as
500 metric tons of water. The figures are higher for Americans
and Finns. The Dutch get by on a little less, and the Japanese
make do with about half that amount. This already indicates to
economic policy makers and business leaders that it is possible
to get by with smaller materials flows without forfeiting quality
of life. But even Japan's forty metric tons per capita per year
cannot be the vision for the entire world. If the rest of humankind attains this level of consumption, we will hardly have the
strength to think much about public finances, globalization, the
pension system, and unemployment. We will be fully occupied
with securing mere survival in an environment becoming ever
more hostile to mankind.

The decisive question my colleagues and I were concerned
with when we first began to think about dematerialization in
1992 at the Wuppertal Institute was: Can we technically organize
the level of prosperity we are accustomed to with a much lower
input of resources?

The surprising and basically enchanting answer is: yes, it can
be done – and especially within the framework of a social market
economy! Our deliberations demonstrated that the economy
would probably even benefit from it. But even within such an aus-
picious frame of reference, any proposal that touches on the basic
pattern of our economic activity will have to be assessed consid-
ering the question of the effects it will have on unemployment

if we dematerialize the economy comprehensively. As far as it is possible to examine and gauge this issue today, the prospects seem so good that we should tackle the realization of this idea. I will discuss this as well in this book.

We are talking about radical dematerialization. This means the attempt to reduce the consumption of materials globally to a sustainable level, which in all probability would neither place an excessive burden on the ecosphere nor damage it in the long term. In concrete terms, we are looking at a period of several decades. The fact that radical dematerialization requires cutting global resource consumption in half makes it clear how much we need to do to reach this goal. This demand will place different burdens on different countries and regions of the world. For if each and every person in the world were to have the right to use the same amount of resources – half of today's amount – that would mean that the old industrialized countries would have to lower their resource consumption by approximately 90% (cf. Fig. 5).

As hard and as drastic this reduction by a factor of ten may sound, our analyses demonstrate that it can indeed be achieved. And I consider the dematerialization involved to be an indispensable prerequisite for launching a sustainable system of economic activity. Since the beginning of the 1990s, I have been calling for the economic systems of the old industrialized countries to dematerialize by at least a factor of ten in the course of the coming decades, which can be achieved only by a new industrial revolution; in the sense that more utility is created in all technical areas using a smaller amount of natural resources. One could also speak of the new 'basic technology' of the 21st century in this context.

The Factor 10 Club I founded in 1994 has dedicated itself to this demand and has published declarations in this regard which,

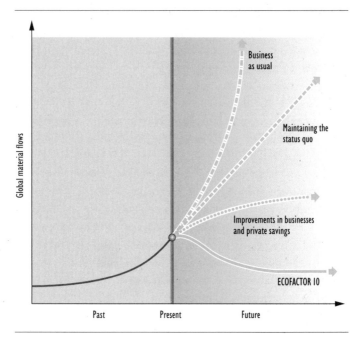

Figure 5   Different progressions of global material flows, projected into
the future

a) assuming unchanged dynamic development, b) assuming that the status quo is
maintained, c) with some improvements and savings (for example, Factor 4),
and d) assuming drastic reduction (at least Factor 10). It is probable that only
the last trajectory will lead to a sustainable economy and thereby also to a
livable planet.

over time, have found an audience. The Club's members are a
group of globally-recognized experts from fifteen countries with
a wealth of practical experience from their positions of leadership
in politics, business, and science, supported by a group of "listen-
ers" which has included, among others, Gro Harlem Brundtland
and Nelson Mandela (see www.factor10-institute.org).

More and more frequently, international resolutions contain terms which are inextricably linked with the new way of viewing our relationship to the environment and the vision it involves, which will be introduced in the course of this book: Factor 10 as well as the concept of the "ecological rucksack," which indicates how much environment we carry around with us, for example when we make a call with a cellphone or work on a laptop computer, and also the metric for ecological economic activity called MIPS (Material Input Per unit of Service).

In January 1997, the then Swedish Minister of the Environment Anna Lindh wrote a letter to her colleagues in Europe, urging them to take the "interesting idea" of Factor 10 into account when implementing the commitments towards protecting the environment they had entered into five years before in Rio de Janeiro.

"Factor 10 spells out the magnitude of the changes which are generally necessary regarding different sectors of industry and different countries. This means that some will even have to go further. The goal is to attain roughly the same level of services which we have today, while using only a fraction of the amount of resources used at present."

To the horror of many, Anna Lindh was later murdered, at a time when it seemed certain she would become the next head of the Swedish government.

Further on, we shall say more about the important concept of "service" which helps us to understand the true utility that people are interested in. In this book, we consider it to be the enrichment of quality of life and well-being that the free choice of services enables individuals to enjoy. Both nature and technology provide us with such services.

The pursuit of an ecologically significant level of dematerialization of today's economic activity whilst still achieving the same level of services for us as consumers, requires that taxes and fees on labor are shifted toward taxation of the consumption of natural resources, making them more expensive. In this book, we demand such a measure, as it would benefit economic development and have positive effects on the labor market.

The purpose of this book is to demonstrate how this dematerialization of economic activity can be brought about. I will present examples, give instructions, draw up checklists, and describe procedures. I have tried to be as close to practical application as the state of research permits, and the state of research permits a lot, for the "Wuppertal Institute for Climate, Environment and Energy," where many of the insights and theses presented in this book were tested and refined, collaborates frequently and successfully with practitioners from the business and political communities. The starting point of the original proposals was an analysis of our way of dealing with natural resources, which I first presented in 1992 and which was then pursued further in the "Material Flows and Resource Management" research group of the newly-founded Wuppertal Institute.

The ecological rucksack and an ecological metric

If it is true that we consume too many natural resources in order to create our prosperity, to make mousetraps and music halls, cars and highways, then that must mean that everything that is produced hauls around a large ballast, a mountain of nature that has been set in motion for this product – in other words, a large ecological rucksack. It is, of course, an invisible rucksack, for I cannot tell by looking at the computer on my desk that its production necessitated shoveling around and thoroughly transforming more than fourteen metric tons of solid nature. It is just as impossible for me to discern that the rucksack is getting heavier by several metric tons as I use the computer. After all, it also needs resources for its use, for example energy. The floor would collapse if this rucksack were filled in my office. But this happens elsewhere, and we never set eyes on it.

Insights emerge which will lead many people to draw surprising conclusions. Who will be left cold when he finds out that – ecologically speaking – the gold ring on a family father's finger weighs more than the van he uses for driving his children around? This is actually the case, for gold is a particularly ecologically "expensive" material because of its elaborate mining methods. On average, every kilogram of industrial product carries approximately thirty kilograms of nature around with it. This means that today, less than 10% of the materials moved around in nature are transformed into useful industrial products in the end.

My demand, therefore, is clear; in the simple language of the media, it is: get rid of the clutter! Use more intelligence, not more material! Intelligence can – and also must – make technology much better. Otherwise, the entire natural basis of our economy will collapse, and there is no other foundation for us to stand on.

If we demand that the economy must be dematerialized and that the ecological rucksacks that belong to it become smaller and lighter, we must also say how one can determine and quantify the size and the material consumption of the rucksacks. And this has to be done not only as simply and unambiguously as possible, but also so that the results are available quickly and with the necessary reliability. In practice, there is not enough time to carry out a scientific study on resource consumption for each individual case. But for practical application, the data need not fulfill all scientific requirements in detail; it is adequate if the information is dependable and "directionally reliable," that is, that even though it may be somewhat imprecise, it is of the correct magnitude and points the people taking action in the right direction. Every designer in industry, every business leader, and every craftsman on the ground must be able to discern alternatives using a simple metric, differentiate between them, and at least move in the right direction. This metric must be designed in such a way that it can be accepted internationally, regardless whether it is to compare the resource efficiency of mousetraps or of Germany's and Japan's economic systems.

The so-called MIPS concept fulfills these requirements. The four letters MIPS are the abbreviation for "Material Input Per unit of Service," and "service" signifies the services which were mentioned above. The material input (MI) includes all the natural raw materials which are moved and used in order to produce, use, transport, and dispose of material goods: sand, water, coal, earth, ores, rapeseed, and trees – in short, everything that we need from the ecosphere.

Energy in the ecological rucksack

In the MIPS concept, the amounts of energy employed are expressed in units of materials and included when determining the MI. To do so, the materials required to make the energy employed are calculated "from the cradle to the grave." The advantage of this procedure is that it is not necessary to work with two different physical units (materials and energy) separately when comparing input of nature per unit of service or utility.

The ecological justification for this procedure lies in the fact that the technical consumption of energy per se does not cause any relevant ecological changes (disregarding massive amounts of radiation in the environment and large explosions). The energy-related cause of some of the most serious dangers to the stability of the ecosphere today – for instance, climate change – lies in the large amount of material consumption per unit of energy made available by technical means as well as losses of energy and energy carriers during their extraction, transportation, and use. Using billions of metric tons of coal, oil, and gas to supply energy is the true environmental problem, not the energy recovered technically in this way. It is the emissions of CO_2, SO_2, and particles of soot, and it is the beaches polluted by oil from spills which cause environmental change, not the energy per se. Saving energy, therefore, is not beneficial to the environment if it comes at the expense of major resource use in relation to the total utility achieved. And finally, harvesting solar energy or geothermal energy can be justified in ecological terms only if the MIPS, the use of material-intensive technology, is small. Optimal use of mass and energy, therefore, can be calculated using MIPS. The smaller the MIPS, the better for the environment.

Some more information to clarify the situation. The MIPS values of the techniques used today to generate electricity – from lignite power plants to nuclear reactors, from photovoltaics to burning rapeseed – vary by a factor of more than fifty. In other words, ecologically speaking, a kilowatt-hour from one electricity source is not necessarily the same as a kilowatt-hour from another source. The German electricity mix is more material-intensive than that of Finland and Austria by a factor of five, for example. Since dematerializing the economy by a factor of ten would entail saving up to 80% of the energy used today, a targeted increase of resource productivity would also result in energy savings.

The MIPS concept relates the total amount of material used (MI), calculated including energy, to the utility we derive from it; after all, it might make sense to tolerate high material input if it yields an exceptionally high amount of utility. For this reason, we calculate the material input "per unit of service" and use this metric. If we did not do so, then it would not make a difference whether just one person or 300 passengers were riding a train. The material input (MI) for moving the train is identical in both cases.

MIPS is the only metric to date which indicates how much utility is derived from a given amount of resources. It provides an index for resource productivity, and we can use the figure calculated to tell whether we are getting closer to the goal of dematerialization.

We have applied the MIPS concept to many examples over the course of the past fifteen years. This brought a number of surprises to light which astonished many ecologically-minded people. One example for this is that producing one kilogram of cotton uses more than 40,000 liters of water in some parts of the world.

Other examples are just as impressive: producing one kilogram of rapeseed means losing almost four kilograms of earth to erosion. Such estimates demonstrate that the German Transrapid magnetic levitation train is significantly superior to the German ICE high-speed train in ecological terms. Using so-called single-use cameras that manufacturers (Eastman Kodak and Fuji, among others) take back free of charge is the most environmentally-friendly way for occasional photographers to take pictures. And the ecological rucksack of packaging paper weighs several times more than that of plastic wrap.

In this book, I would like to tell the story of how to approach things in a practical way, how designers can create dematerialized products, how to calculate MIPS, and what ecological rucksacks look like in detail. Of course, there are theoretical sections which elucidate why a technically intelligent service society is identical to a dematerialized society, why increasing the resource productivity of products leads to detecting new market niches, and why wise ecological policy creates jobs using a market-based approach.

In all likelihood, I will have to leave more questions open than the reader would like. For this I beg your forgiveness.

How we manage resources

When resources are discussed in policy circles today, the debate almost always centers on the demand to use them sparingly and preserve them so that we do not deprive future generations of the foundations upon which their lives depend. Some environmental experts even demand that we stop using "non-renewable" resources as quickly as possible. This would include, for example, sand and ores, limestone and granite. I consider this approach wrong. The goal should not be to preserve resources in their natural deposits, but to minimize the material flows caused by technology as quickly as possible. This means that the amount of raw materials which mankind sets in motion day by day and changes physically or chemically must be reduced. They are – in several respects – the triggers of ecological changes, and of climate change as well. From this perspective, there is fundamentally no difference between non-renewable resources and resources which grow back biologically, or which – like water – move through natural cycles. Put simply: the amount of raw materials is the primary problem, not the kind of raw materials.

When the issue is to determine the limits of environmentally-friendly use of non-renewable resources, including energy carriers, then the decisive criterion is not that these substances will be depleted at a particular point in time, but rather that the changes in the ecosphere which are linked to their use and depletion. In this vein, it is to be expected that burning coal and mineral oil will shift ecological equilibriums dramatically long before the deposits are depleted.

If the goal is to make the limits of sustainable use of soils measurable, then decisive criteria include both avoiding erosion and retaining the soils' ecological functionality. Soils must be able to fulfill their purpose as "reservoirs" of water to lessen the temperature differences between day and night and to feed sources and groundwater flows with potable water. Sealing soils makes it impossible for them to do so, and soil compaction by means of gigantic machinery for agriculture and forestry limits this capacity significantly as well. Retaining ecological functionality of soils also includes preserving the appropriate combination of nutrients and minerals the indigenous plants of a particular region need to grow.

If the goal is to make the limits of the sustainable use of biomass – plants and animals – measurable, then the decisive criterion is to create locally appropriate products if at all possible and not to harvest more than can grow back under natural conditions. The distance to the consumer should be as short as possible.

The effects of overfertilization and application of excessive amounts of liquid manure have been written about extensively. In addition, however, resource consumption per metric ton of products derived from biomass is of decisive importance. It should be as small as possible. For example, this implies that farmland is prepared and worked with the smallest possible amount of earth movement and compaction, and that products are processed, stored, and packaged as efficiently as possible. In other words: the resource productivity of the means employed should be maximized.

According to analyses prepared by Gunter Pauli, up to 90% of the biomass produced on agricultural land, especially on plantations, is lost – an enormous waste of resources. For comparison, we turn to the mineral oil industry. There, the relationship is just the opposite: more than 90% of the crude oil produced is transformed into salable products. And there definitely are chemical and biochemical processes which would help us to employ biomass more efficiently. This aspect is especially important because to date, it has not been taken into account in discussions about the "Green Revolution," genetic engineering, or the use of chemicals in agriculture. In principle, the problem is not the production of more and more biomass, but rather the intelligent use of what is available in any case. Pauli gives examples: many trees are cut down only for cellulose for producing paper. However, only 35% of the wood mass is cellulose, the remainder is considered waste. Using the traditional methods for making beer, 90% of the water used never ends up in the beer bottle, and waste biomass is landfilled or, at best, used as cattle feed. Pauli's conclusion: "That is the new Green Revolution: making more products from the same amount of input."

From old to new environmental policy

The number one environmental policy goal of the Federal Republic of Germany is to make the economy sustainable in ecological terms. The question arises whether a law that requires our economy above all to close the loops of material flows can make sense at all. This is the prime goal of the "Closed Substance Cycle and Waste Management Act." I would say it does not. If we do not stop the torrents of resources that are currently flowing into our production of goods but force them into cycles which require additional transportation, new resources, and even more energy, we will experience material "congestion" of our economy in the end – with inestimable ecological consequences.

The fact that – as mentioned above – approximately 70% of man-made solid material flows cannot be managed in closed loops because of technical reasons itself speaks against closing loops as the guiding principle: a large part of the flows never enter the production "cycle" because it is simply mining waste, overburden, or other material which is moved – but not used – to produce goods. In addition, many materials are dispersed in the environment during their use, for example, paints and varnishes, and the carbon in energy carriers such as coal, tar sands, and mineral oil is burned to CO_2. Both make it impossible to close loops, at least within reasonable economic and ecological limits.

Let us take a closer look at the world of material recycling. First of all, it can be demonstrated for many cases that this type of recycling is very expensive, ecologically speaking, in terms of resource consumption. In addition, when assessing recycling, one must always take into consideration that in each loop around the cycle, more or less mass is lost, because no technical recycling process can reclaim 100% of the materials employed. In other words, efficiency is always less than 100%. So even in the case of aluminum recycling, which is often mentioned as an example for the high efficiency of raw material recycling, a few percent of the aluminum is lost in the scrap during the recycling process. If a recycling process reclaims 90% of the raw material, that means that after fifteen cycles, only approximately 20% of the original mass remains. In addition, even the best collection system cannot feed all the material which was originally used in the economy into the recycling process (particularly if it is not worth much in economic terms). Not even gold comes out of the recycling process with 100% reclaimed. If we assume that 75% of the raw materials are fed back into the recycling process, then, after fifteen cycles, almost 99% of the originally used mass have disappeared.

If our goal is to make the economy sustainable, we must slow down resource flows while retaining our level of prosperity. Closing loops itself does not effect any relevant slowing of the speed at which resources flow through the economy, and most countries cannot even afford material recycling – unless the poorest of the poor take on an important part of the work. Many people live off, and on, the landfills where the leftovers of the rich are dumped. In Jakarta, for example, plastics are officially removed from the garbage and recycled; the city government supports this practice which provides a modest livelihood for many. But even where the material dug out of the leavings of the prosperous cannot be resold, the reuse of industrial products has a long tradition. Packaging materials of all kind – barrels, cardboard boxes, plastics – are used for all manner of purposes, for example, for roofing. In terms of the global material flows, however, this form of recycling is a drop in the ocean. It may be important for the people who benefit from it, but can occur only where poverty leaves no other alternative.

That means even if the Closed Substance Cycle and Waste Management Act does ease the burden on the environment for the moment, it is not the enthusiastic departure into the future we need.

In a nutshell, up until now environmental policy has been going in the wrong direction and will miss the goal of sustainability remains because it has not recognized the main problem which lies in the movement of material flows. A future-oriented environmental policy must improve resource productivity decisively and must not get bogged down in the details of individual analyses, such as return systems for beverage containers, intercepting "hazardous materials," and recycling waste.

The old type of environmental policy follows the principle: people produce, eat, drink, wash, fly – more or less without a care in the world. And at the end, wastewater treatment plants, filters, and catalytic converters intercept some of the harmful substances, at a high cost. The solid remains of the resources flowing through our society are collected in armies of ugly garbage containers, which are emptied in billions of hours of labor on specially-designed vehicles that themselves use a lot of resources and make a lot of noise.

You will have noticed that I have become somewhat impatient with conventional environmental policy, even though I myself was responsible for the development and implementation of environmental protection in the German Chemicals Act twenty-five years ago.

Even so, this old-style "protection of the environment" did provide for a few hundred thousand jobs in the economy and in government agencies controlling it – even if these jobs were not productive in the end. But environmental protection of this kind has become too ineffective and too expensive. It does not serve its purpose if the goal is sustainability.

New-style environmental policy works in a different way: from the beginning, people use less water, raw materials, and energy – and not because they are limiting their activities and forgoing quality of life, but thanks to elegant technology, good ideas, and new product design. Controlling hazardous substances remains largely untouched by this.

Finally, an example for where new ideas are needed: a travel agency will issue a customer traveling by train from Wuppertal, Germany, to Paris, France, and back nine (!) pieces of heavy paper in the form of tickets and seat reservations, about six by twenty centimeters in size. In addition, the traveler receives hard copies of the train connections for the trips out and back, each about twelve by twenty centimeters. That adds up to a piece of heavy paper measuring seventy-eight by twenty centimeters. If we assume that Deutsche Bahn, the German rail service, has 100,000 passengers per day who are supplied with such materials, then this results in a total amount of approximately eighty kilometers of heavy paper twenty centimeters wide. At about ten grams of paper per passenger, this yields around 1000 kilograms or one metric ton. As we will see below, we have to multiply this weight with the "material input factor" (MIF) of paper to cover the total amount of natural resources employed for this purpose. The material input factor of paper is fifteen metric tons per metric ton of paper, not including water. Altogether, that totals a little less than 3500 metric tons per year for tickets issued by Deutsche Bahn, which corresponds roughly to the weight of 3000 VW Rabbits.

It should not be very difficult to improve this situation by a factor of ten. Airlines might be in a position to give advice, even though they, too, still have ample room for improvement.

When we buy something – a car, a scarf, a clock, a container of yogurt – we usually don't do this just to own the product and show it to other people. We want to use our purchases; we spend money on something to satisfy a need. We acquire cars for mobility, we buy scarves to warm our necks, etc. What matters in the end is not the product itself, but the service which it performs for us – in the case of the clock, to show us the time, and in the case of the yogurt, to satisfy our need for food.

As early as the 1970s, Erich Jantsch determined that the most important feature of a product is the service it performs for its owner. Jantsch differentiated between functions on the one hand and material products as well as immaterial services which can perform these functions on the other.

"Regarding the functional criteria, the question is how well a given product performs a function, compared with other available products which may employ completely different technologies, and how the introduction of a product affects the system of human life – for example, the influence the technology of the motor vehicle has on life in big cities, compared with subways, monorails, bicycles, rolling sidewalks, or other forms and combinations of urban transportation technology."

This quotation contains at least three important concepts. Firstly: if it is not a question of the product *per se*, but of the function it performs, then it is clear that we can choose the product which performs the task for us best and cheapest among many which perform the same function in principle. Secondly: provided that appropriate information is available, when we make that choice, we can take into consideration which product both performs the service and was produced in the most environmentally-friendly way, that is, which product is the most eco-intelligent. And thirdly: all this means that it is not relevant whether we own a product. The actually important thing is the function, not ownership of a product that performs that function.

Aristotle was already aware of this more than 2000 years ago, as this quotation demonstrates: "True wealth comes from using things, not from owning them."

Focus on function

Our goal must be to seek the most ecologically and economically effective ways to perform a particular function, to satisfy a particular need. This is crucial for environmental policy, because it points the way out of the simple, but fruitless alternative "buy or do without" and encourages us to look for ways in which comparable services (performing functions) can be provided with substantially lower use of resources.

Using the example of the need for "keeping the lawn short," we shall illustrate several practical options for the consumer. One can purchase a lawnmower for this purpose, spending more or less money on it, depending on whether it is powered by electricity, a gasoline engine, or human muscles. Some luxury models even have a seat for the operator and automatically collect the cuttings. Each individual version has its own use of resources.

Instead of purchasing such equipment, one can also commission a gardening business to mow the lawn several times a year as needed: the gardener then arrives with the company's lawnmower, the use of which is included in the price. A third possibility is to join together with neighbors and share a lawnmower. A fourth solution would be to have a sheep graze on the grass from time to time (not a goat, as it would tear out the roots as well). Finally, the fifth possibility would be the so-called "zero option," namely simply letting the grass grow along with the flowers sown with it, and removing the dried grass at the end of the winter season.

These five possible alternatives for performing the function "mowing the lawn" are entirely different in terms of their natural resource use. The first possibility is still the most common and the one with the highest resource use by far, with the exception of the muscle-powered variety of lawnmowers. In the second option, the gardening company's equipment is used intensively, its "capacity utilization" is relatively high. As professional machinery is usually designed to be more robust than equipment for private use, its rucksack is often larger, as will become clear below. The MIPS value we prefer, on the other hand, tends to be smaller, because such equipment is more durable and needs fewer repairs and resources per unit of service. What is more, this solution also creates jobs.

Assuming the professional equipment lasts for ten years, its resource productivity increases substantially compared with the first solution. In the third option, if five families share a lawnmower, the MIPS value is less than the first option by a factor of about three or four.

The important thing is which path is used in each particular case to reduce the amount of material used to achieve the same utility. While the second and third options improve the resource productivity of utility by using the equipment better (the intensity of its use is increased) – that is, by organizational means – the fourth and fifth solutions take different approaches.

In the case of the sheep, the resource inputs to be allocated to eating grass are a good deal lower than in the first three options. In addition, the sheep transforms ("recycles") the grass (otherwise "waste" that would require disposal) into biomass in the form of meat and wool. In other words, MIPS approaches zero. One can save money and gain biomass, a win-win option. As we are talking about recycling creating win-win situations, I would like to remind the reader that since time immemorial, pigs and ducks have been kept as "leftover refiners." Why this practice is not more widespread in rural areas – for example, to reuse waste from restaurants profitably – is a mystery to me.

In the fifth case, resource productivity improves via a personal decision to change behavior. The material intensity per square meter of cut grass is lower than in the case of a lawnmower of one's own by at least a factor of one hundred! This kind of provision of utility can be called a "zero option." The city governments of Hamburg, Germany, and many other cities practice this option.

Of course, the last option requires a different way of looking at things: if you consider an English lawn a must, perhaps not even because you find it prettier than a flowering meadow, but because you feel it necessary to enhance your social status vis-à-vis your neighbors and other people in general, then uncut grass with flowers will not be an attractive option.

Voluntary zero options are always characterized by high resource productivity and financial savings. In our case, preserving the diversity of flowers, butterflies, and insects is also an interesting aspect. From my point of view, bans and requirements are not a good way to effect zero options for saving resources. Not only does it cost a lot of money to administer them, they also curtail free decision-making and self-reliance. I always prefer installing economic incentives to guide people to save resources.

Let us sum up briefly what has been said thus far in this chapter: we purchase products not primarily in order to own them but because they are useful for us and provide services. This fact permits us to benefit both in ecological and economic terms: if only the utility of products is sold (by renting, leasing etc.), they will be used more efficiently, fewer goods will be needed and produced, and they will be more durable because of the service providers' own economic interests, as they make money on providing utility.

Saving money on materials rather than on personnel, and offering more services instead – in this way, the economy will become more competitive because of the lower costs, and at the same time, jobs are created. The motto should be "taking care of the lawn" rather than "selling lawnmowers." In a different case: "providing mobility" rather than "selling cars." The question arises how one can encourage people who are seeking utility to take advantage – if at all possible – of services which I would call "eco-intelligent." What I mean by this is satisfying a defined need – or a bundle of needs – at market prices by means of products (so-called service machines), which in turn can be considered to be objects, tools, machines, buildings, and infrastructures which provide as many different services as possible during their entire operative life at market prices and with minimum possible use of materials, energy, land area, waste, transportation, packaging, and hazardous substances.

Two new concepts

From an ecological point of view, it would be ideal if we could buy services in pure form, without any material help. In that case, we would not place any strain on the environment at all. But that is not how things are: a service-based society, too, needs natural resources, and it should use them as productively as it possibly can. For that to succeed, two things to which I shall now turn my attention must be taken into account.

Firstly, we must know how large a burden a product or a service puts on the environment, the weight of its ecological rucksack. This information is needed to make different products and services comparable and to reveal starting points for technical optimization. For example, only if drill manufacturers know that for every gram of copper that is part of the machine, 500 grams of natural resources must be used, will they begin to think about saving copper drastically. And only if craftspeople know that an electronically-controlled drill contains components whose production, as a rule, requires very high resource consumption, will it occur to them to ponder whether a machine without electronic components might do the job as well.

Secondly, we need a goal for our efforts to save resources. How much resource use is too much? This piece of information is more important than it appears at first glance. Why shouldn't we save resources wherever possible?

The answer is: because then, we might miss the goal drastically, in whichever direction. Saving "too much" would not damage the environment, to be sure, but perhaps it would make us restrict our own lives to such an extent that we would never be in a position to strike a course which could be maintained in the long run. The danger is greater that we might sit back too early when it comes to taking care of the ecosphere because we think we have done enough. And what is worse: if we set our goals too modestly, we may put a series of simple ways of easing the strain on nature into practice without becoming aware of the fact that we are not reaching the actual goals. If the members of an environmentally-conscious family know that their natural resource consumption is too large by a factor of four, then they might sell their second car and buy bus tickets instead. This one measure might be enough to reach the goal in the field of transportation. But if they know that their resource use is too high by a factor of ten, then this simple solution will not meet the goal. In this case, it will be necessary for them to reflect fundamentally on their lifestyle and the kind of technologies they use.

This, however, is the crucial point. If we want to reach the goal of a sustainable lifestyle and economic system, then we must know if it is sufficient to strive towards solutions that fit into our existing structures and customs in the economy, transportation, and leisure time, or whether we have to change these structures and customs. If the latter is the case, then we must approach the problem in a different way to begin with. If we don't, then there is the danger that we spend many years on efforts to make many small improvements in our way of dealing with natural resources, invest a lot of time and energy, and in the end will have to admit that the ecosphere surrounding us is still degenerating. Mountain climbers are familiar with this situation: the peak you are trying to scale recedes into the distance, beyond reach, when you thought for hours that you had it right in front of you, and then, when you get there, you realize that you are atop a small foothill that concealed the view of the actual goal.

How much too large is the ecological rucksack of the industrialized countries' economic system? By how much do they have to dematerialize? My answer is: by at least a factor of ten. This will be explained in detail below, but we are well advised to focus steadfastly on this goal from the beginning. It is challenging, but not unattainable. For example, the material input for electricity from wind power is smaller by a factor of fifty than that of burning lignite for the same purpose. And in Haellefors, Sweden, a company succeeded in reducing the consumption of

cooling agents for boring and cutting metal components by a
factor of 18,000.

Ecological rucksacks

The idea of rucksacks came to me when I was thinking about
how best to proceed by way of calculation in order to grasp the
amount of nature captured in every material object (Fig. 6). The
problem lies in the fact that the weight of classical clothes pegs
says little about how much wood had to be removed from the
forest to manufacture the components. Neither does the weight
of the steel springs give me any information about the mining
waste that had to be moved from its original geological location
to make the ore available, or about how much transportation was
necessary, or how much resource use was involved in constructing the blast furnaces for producing the steel. And that is only
the beginning of the story.

It is, however, possible, to trace all the steps of the process back
from the mousetrap to the point where the natural raw materials
were originally extracted, that is, "to the cradle" of the product.
One can trace this path back "in material terms" by unraveling
the process chains involved. In addition, one can trace it back
"geographically," that is, ask which country or which region the
individual materials are from. If you are interested in ecological
trade balances from this point of view, you will notice that the
ecological rucksacks of imports into the European Union have
increased substantially (Fig. 7). While it is true that we have succeeded in lowering the environmental burden per unit of gross
domestic product in Europe, we have shifted the ecological costs
to the developing countries.

The ecological rucksack is defined as the sum of all masses

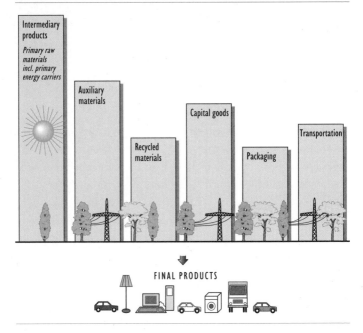

Figure 6   Packing an ecological rucksack

Many more materials are needed on the way to a final product than the product itself contains. Raw materials such as iron ore and coal are used to make unrefined iron, which is then processed together with other resources (and energy) to make the steel for constructing a product. This covers only the part of the ecological rucksack in the column on the left. The other columns increase its rucksack further. Typically, industrial products carry rucksacks weighing 30 times more than the products themselves.

moved in nature and out of nature – material input (MI) – in metric tons (kilograms or grams) all the way to the ready-for-sale product in metric tons (kilograms or grams), minus the weight of the product itself. In other words, the calculation stretches all the way "from the cradle" to the finished product.

In other words, the ecological rucksack also includes the

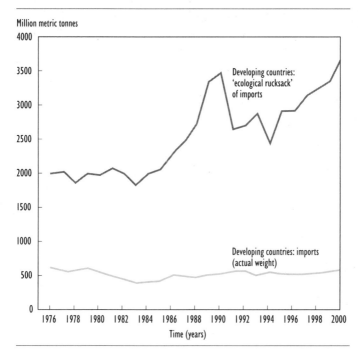

Million metric tonnes

Figure 7   Ecological rucksacks of imports
The ecological rucksacks of imports have increased since the mid-1980s and
have become much larger than the amount of imports themselves.

masses of the energy carriers used as well as the proportions of
the masses of the facilities that produced the electricity necessary
for manufacturing the product. The same applies for heat from
solar technology or geothermal sources used in the process.

In doing so, the ecological rucksack also points to the useless
part of resource use during the production of goods. It is the
invisible part of goods, and if you weigh the goods themselves,
this part is missing completely.

The rucksack should be as light as possible, but often, it is astoundingly heavy, as the following example, authored by Eija Koski from the Finnish Association of Nature Protection in Helsinki, shows:

Mirja's weighty morning

Mirja wakes up and straps her watch weighing 12.5 kilograms on her wrist, pulls on her 30-kilogram jeans, switches on her coffee maker weighing 52 kilograms, and sips her brew from a mug weighing in at 1.5 kilograms. After tying her jogging shoes (3.5 kilograms), she cycles to her office on her bicycle that weighs 400 kilograms. When she has arrived, she boots-up her computer (several metric tons) and makes her first phone call using a telephone weighing 25 kilograms. Mirja's day has begun – just like any other day. But this time, with ecological rucksacks.

The ecological rucksack of services which are performed by using goods can be expressed as follows: the ecological rucksack of a service is the sum of the prorated rucksacks of the technical means used (for example, equipment, vehicles, and buildings), plus the sum of the prorated consumption of materials and energy while the technical means employed are being used.

Ecological rucksacks remain unchanged if a product is not used. They reflect something akin to the interference in the environment on account of a product or service and permit a comparison of goods and services of any kind in ecological terms. Information about ecological rucksacks permits us to dematerialize the design and manufacture of products or services. In this way, the search for lighter rucksacks can begin, with the goal of putting goods on the market that are more eco-intelligent.

The ecological price, or the true price of things

When you buy a product, you pay the retail price, which is the sum of all the individual prices for raw and processed materials, intermediate products, supplies, and production itself (wages including non-wage labor costs) as well as the retailer's profit margin. If you were to pay a real price – real from the perspective of sustainability – you would also have to pay for the rucksack introduced above. However, instead of quoting a monetary price for the so-called ecological price, we would like to specify a weight, namely the sum of the ecological rucksack and the product – the car – itself. If we use this method, the ecological price encompasses the entire material input or the added material value which accrues from the cradle of the raw materials to the ready-for-sale and ready-for-service product.

Each product has its traditional price – in a particular currency – and its ecological price in kilograms of nature. If a retailer were to indicate both prices, the price tag for a mid-range car would look roughly like this:

Purchase price: 31,000 euros
Empty weight: 1300 kg
Ecological price: 40,300 kilograms of nature (non-renewable resources)

This information could also be provided in another way:

Purchase price: 31,000 euros

In other words: 24 euros per kilogram of car

And 77 cents per kilogram of nature (non-renewable resources)

Whether or not such information on the price tag influences consumers' purchasing decisions remains an open question at present, not least because there is a confusing multitude of environmental labels, many of which are difficult to understand.

Material input factors – MIF

Material input factors (also called rucksack factors) are used in order to calculate rucksacks in a straightforward way. MIFs are the result of detailed calculations of the movements of masses for providing individual raw materials and intermediate products – calculated from the cradle onwards – and are given in kilograms per kilogram. The results of our analyses show that MIFs are surprisingly large for metals. For instance, the rucksack for gold has a material input factor of 540,000. That means that for each gram of gold, 540,000 grams of raw materials (not including water) must be removed from their natural locations and processed. 540,000 grams – that is more than half a metric ton per gram of gold. In contrast, the MIF for glass is only two kilograms per kilogram. So the difference between MIF values is quite substantial. If we know the composition of a product and its total weight, we can calculate its rucksack quickly and easily.

Christa Liedtke and her team at the Wuppertal Institute calculated the material input of many materials in the 1990s. Some of the figures available today are presented in the appendix. The values given there reflect results from many countries. They are averages and will certainly be improved in the future.

When analyzing the figures, it becomes apparent that secondary (recycled) materials can be much better in ecological terms than primary ones whose raw materials were removed from nature. In the case of copper, for example, the relationship of the "primary" MIF to the "secondary" MIF is 500 to 10. In other words, simply replacing primary copper with recycled copper corresponds to a dematerialization by a factor of fifty. However, this requires that the copper gained from raw materials originally has already served its purpose in the first phase of its use.

Five different rucksacks

At the Wuppertal Institute, we divided the naturally-occurring raw materials into five categories, for practical reasons. We calculated and listed the ecological rucksacks separately in each of these five categories, and the goal of dematerialization by a factor of ten which is promoted in this book must be attained in each and every category. In other words, the MIF categories will not be offset against one another. The five MIF categories are the following:

1. Abiotic (inanimate) raw materials: firstly, solid mineral or inorganic raw materials derived from mining, smelters, and other extraction procedures such as rock, ores, and sand; secondly, fossil energy carriers such as coal, mineral oil, and natural gas which are predominantly used for power generation; thirdly, masses of rock and earth which are merely moved in order to extract abiotic raw materials; and fourthly, earth which has been moved, for example overburden. The latter includes all movements of soil and

earth for constructing and maintaining infrastructures (buildings, roads, rail networks).

2. We include in the category of biotic (animate) raw materials plant-based biomass from cultivating the soil, in other words, all plants which have been harvested, picked, gathered, or used in another way. This category also encompasses animal biomass, which, however, is calculated in units of the plant-based inputs which were necessary in order to produce them (the grass eaten by the cow is counted, not the cow herself). Biotic raw materials also include biomass from domains which are not cultivated, that is, wild animals, fish, and wild plants (including trees).

3. Movements of earth in agriculture and forestry occur by mechanical means for cultivation as well as by erosion. These masses are important because movements of natural resources on account of agriculture and forestry, too, trigger fundamental ecological changes. The amount and frequency of movements of earth serve as indicators for the degree of ecological influence. Since the volume of earth moved by mechanical means (by plowing, harrowing, etc.) per harvest season is extraordinarily large in relation to the harvest itself (the ratio is more than one hundred to one), in most cases, we use erosion as the indicator for the extent of movements of earth for soil-related production in agriculture and forestry. Movements of soil by plowing and harrowing are not incorporated directly in this rucksack. So, strictly speaking, this indicator does not include a mass flow moved by technical means – namely by mechanical cultivation – but a flow which occurs as a consequence: erosion. For this and other reasons, reducing the amount of earth moved by mechanical means by a factor of ten is an urgent imperative. Alternative methods of cultivation are already available today.

4. Water is taken into account in calculations whenever it is
   actively removed from nature, that is, by technical means.
   This also includes damming. So water that flows through
   a water wheel on a natural course of a stream or a river, or
   water that is moved by a ship's propeller is not included.
   It makes sense to differentiate according to the source of
   water: surface water, groundwater, and deep groundwater
   (fossil). Any exchange between these three water reserves
   takes place only with a time lag; in addition, they have
   different ecological functions. Deep groundwater, for
   example, renews itself so slowly that, applying a human
   scale, it is practically a non-renewable resource. For more
   detailed analyses, the designated use of the water is also
   documented. We consider the following categorization
   useful: of water as a chemical raw material, hydropower,
   water for cooling, water for irrigation, draining or
   diversion of water, water as a means of transportation, and
   mechanical use of water.

5. Air and its components are considered material inputs if
   they are actively extracted by man, dissociated into their
   chemical components, or changed in terms of their chemical
   properties (for example, NH_3 as a base for fertilizer from
   N_2 in the air). In particular, this includes air necessary for
   combustion and air used for processes involving chemical
   and physical conversion. In each case, only the weight
   of the changed components of the air, for example the
   oxygen needed for combustion, is counted. Air merely
   moved mechanically (by windmills, air used for cooling,
   compressed air, and ventilation) is not taken into account,
   even though, strictly speaking, it was moved by technical
   means.

For industrial products, it often turns out that only the categories "abiotic raw materials" and "water" contribute meaningfully to the end result.

And why this categorization? The five different material flows have very different impacts on the environment, and in addition, their sizes differ greatly. For example, most industrial products consume ten to twenty times as much water as solid masses. This means that by saving water alone, the factor of ten can often be attained relatively easily. That would make sense, of course, and would certainly be in the spirit of the MIPS concept. But it could also tempt us to limit our efforts to remove stresses from the ecosphere to partial material flows which are technically easy and particularly financially rewarding to minimize. This would only lead to partially optimal or even suboptimal solutions.

We divide the ecological rucksack into five partial rucksacks to demonstrate that a monolithic view is not helpful when it comes to removing burdens from the ecosphere, but that the entire breadth of ecologically relevant interferences must be taken into account.

Factor 10

In 1995, I had the pleasure of meeting an extraordinarily intelligent citizen of Hong Kong, a music teacher. Seldom have I met a more enthusiastic proponent of the kind of progress exemplified by the old industrialized countries, as role models for the other, much larger part of the roughly six billion people on this planet. She was practically glowing with zeal in showing us the breathtaking progress her city was making in housing millions of people in huge apartment blocks. The old boating district of Aberdeen with its population of 40,000 had disappeared overnight. The people who had previously lived there, now up on the twentieth floor: what might they be dreaming about now?

More than two billion Chinese, Indians, and Indonesians are using all the means at their disposal to emulate – as quickly as possible – the leap into material prosperity they have seen the classic industrialized countries make. Everything we see on television is broadcast by satellite to their homes as well and drummed into their minds from gigantic billboards every time they walk through town. As a result, their material goals are clearly defined.

While we are harboring doubts whether our economic system is appropriate for the new millennium, the people there are still copying our patterns with relatively unbroken enthusiasm. What other options do they have besides more or less following in our footsteps? If their efforts prove successful, then the stress on the ecosphere, which is not sustainable as it is, will be multiplied, because the number of people emulating our lifestyle makes up about four-fifths of humanity. That is the bad news for the environment. But there is also good news.

While in the industrialized countries, people are beginning to think about a sustainable economic system while they are at an unsustainable level of resource consumption, many of the countries we do not count among the "old" industrialized countries are starting out from a level of resource consumption per capita that still leaves some room to maneuver – scope for progress in the classical sense of the word, but also for skipping the detour through the ecological mistakes of the industrialized countries from the outset and taking a more sustainable route instead.

A range of possibilities opens up, at least theoretically, but hopefully also in a practical sense. The MIPS concept can help determine the ecologically superior alternative even where the desire for prosperity is still tied in with satisfying people's basic needs, thereby drawing attention away from concern for the eco-sphere. But particularly in this international field, it becomes apparent that the MIPS concept, as we suspected, is not a panacea.

In shaping people's well-being and security, different countries currently display very different patterns of natural resource use; even within "poor" countries, the differences can be astounding. At all times and in all places, rich and poor seem to exist. Some of the starkest differences today are to be seen precisely in the poorer countries.

Factor 10 takes these differences into account. The concept intentionally incorporates a certain amount of leeway for thresh-old countries and developing countries so that they can still increase their per capita consumption of natural resources on the way to economic prosperity.

The number ten is the result of a simple back-of-the-envelope calculation: the current level of resource use of all of mankind taken together is not sustainable. Numerous studies suggest that cutting resource use in half would ease the burden on the eco-sphere – an urgently needed step. That is the call for a factor of two. If we then distribute the possibly still feasible amount of resource consumption evenly among all people, which interna-tional justice would demand, then the industrialized countries must reduce their consumption by much more than just a factor of two, while poor countries would still be permitted to increase their resource use.

By how much do the industrialized countries have to reduce their resource use? If all of them are to attain similar levels of consumption after a phase of adaptation and relearning, then the industrialized countries must arrive at approximately one-tenth of their current use. One-tenth must be enough for us, the rich. That is the call for a factor of ten.

For China, a rough calculation would go something like this: China's population is approximately the same size as that of all the old industrialized countries put together, or 20% of all people. The country's per capita resource consumption is about 20% of that in rich countries. If the rich, then, were to reduce their resource consumption on average by a factor of ten, then China could double its resource use, and the global goal of cutting resource use in half would still be met – provided that other poor countries are not even poorer than China, therefore requiring more room for growth. It is also conceivable that developing countries first go beyond the scope provided by the Factor 10 concept for their resource consumption, but decrease again over the course of the following years by improving resource productivity to reach the level to which they are "entitled."

In any case, it would be unrealistic to believe that our theoretical discussions could prevent developing countries from continuing along the path that promises them the material prosperity of the "rich" countries. Only if we succeed in demonstrating practical ways of creating comparable prosperity with substantially lower levels of natural resource consumption would people in developing countries have another model worth taking seriously. They would presumably take it seriously in particular if they got the impression that this is the new, "modern" way of having an important voice in the circle of the world's economic powers. But it may transpire in the near future that the natural resources necessary for the great leap into a western-style consumer society are simply not available. Recent developments in the prices of oil, gold, cement, and steel indicate this in any case. According to the June 27, 2006 edition of the *Herald Tribune*, these commodity prices have doubled since 2002.

The countries exporting raw materials would face

disadvantages due to dematerialization. As the Factor 10 concept is founded on cutting the global resource flows in the economy in half, the countries exporting raw materials would have to accept a loss of 50% of their exports, not 90%, which would correspond to a factor of ten! This drop in exports by half would accrue over the course of decades, which should provide ample time to help the economy adapt by means of structural changes at the domestic level and a shifting of economic activity to other sectors.

If the industrialized countries are to become role models for developing countries regarding a new, sustainable type of prosperity, they would have to turn away from the OECD countries' current practice of economic aid almost completely. Today's economic aid involves exporting techniques and products of the generation of high resource consumption and promoting the production of such products and the corresponding infrastructures. But that is the wrong path to take. How profound the necessary change would be becomes apparent if one looks at how our mass media currently value state visits. The more locomotives, automobile factories, machine tools, and power plants are sold on such occasions, the more jubilant the hymns of praise to the heads of government and the business leaders traveling with them – a nothing less than grotesque error of judgment from an ecological point of view.

Can patterns of behavior ingrained so deeply be transformed in time? I don't know. But I believe that they can.

In a nutshell

Every material product can be produced only by interfering in the ecosphere, by setting material flows in motion. At least the amount of material that comprises the product itself must be moved, but as a rule, that is not enough. Every material product carries an ecological rucksack around with it. It consists of the raw materials that also had to be moved in order to manufacture the product. The same holds for almost all services. Even if non-material services are provided, they require transportation, aids and appliances, or other material objects which are linked to material flows. Services, too, carry ecological rucksacks.

The ecological rucksacks must be reduced in size. The industrialized countries must dematerialize their economic systems by a factor of ten within thirty to fifty years. If today's "rich" industrialized countries make this goal a reality, it will permit today's "poorer" countries to increase their resource use until they reach the same per capita consumption as the industrialized countries, while still cutting the material flows of the world's economy in half. This global factor of two is the minimum goal that we must attain to make the world's economy sustainable.

3 The Ecological Metric

I introduced the idea of an ecological rucksack in order to assess whether we actually pay the real price of products, from an ecological point of view, and therefore also pay for the service we receive by using them. I would now like to ask the following question: when we compare two products whose use provides us with the same utility, can the ecological rucksack alone help us decide which of the two goods is better from an ecological perspective?

Oddly enough, the answer is no, because the ecological rucksack takes only the genesis of an industrial product into account, that is, everything that happens from the cradle of the resources for individual components to their assembly as a ready-to-use and ready-for-sale product which, of course, still needs to be transported to the store where we finally buy it and take it home – without, however, having to haul the ecological rucksack away as well.

But a product's actual life just begins at that point: after all, we spend our money on them in order to gain utility from them after buying them. That is their *raison d'être*, and when we utilize a product, many additional resources are necessary. We notice this fact especially when we have to pay for them – for example, when we buy gasoline for our cars or pay our electricity bills.

If we want to enjoy the utility of a car, for example, we have to do more than fill the tank. For the car to function as a means of transportation, we also have to take care of insurance, taxes, oil, batteries, tires, car polish, spare parts, and snow chains in the winter. The costs and the labor for consequential costs are to be found neither in the car's purchase price nor in its ecological rucksack. They cannot be easily estimated in total, simply because the information is difficult – or impossible – to come by.

Nonetheless, I would like to attempt a first estimate of the costs, and this calculation will be easy to follow. Let us assume that the car uses seven liters of gasoline per hundred kilometers and is driven 100,000 kilometers. Based on a gasoline price of approximately 1.20 euros per liter, gasoline alone amounts to more than 8400 euros, and the additional costs – for car wash, repairs, inspection, taxes, insurance – add up roughly to at least the same amount again. After eight to ten years of use, this results in the price of a small car – and in theory, it has been driven only 100,000 kilometers!

If we set the purchase price in relation to the kilometers driven or the length of time the car is used, then the costs per kilometer or per month may be very high at the beginning, but they decrease as the vehicle gets older because the purchase price is amortized over time. This process ends, however, when repairs become more frequent and more expensive. So, economically speaking, the durability of the things we use matters a lot. As a result, wise consumers can compare offers on the market only if they are aware of the total costs per utility unit or per service unit which accrue during the useful life of a product, and take them into account. A car that is more expensive at the outset and is also heavier may turn out to be more economical than a cheaper and lighter one, but this is not necessarily the case. This has been called the Rolls-Royce effect. This coinage indicates that products with a long life span that are substantially more expensive than others at the time of purchase may be cheaper overall when their total performance is taken into account.

Of course, this holds for the amount of resources used per unit of performance over the life span as well. An energy-saving light bulb, for instance, costs an average of five to eight times as much as a traditional light bulb. The energy-saving bulb, however, lasts ten times as long as the conventional one and produces five times as much light per unit of electricity. The higher purchase price is worth it, in other words, because in this case, it is for the cheaper service-fulfillment machine, and that is what matters.

In order to indicate the true, economically meaningful total price of a product (which, unfortunately, remains hypothetical and practically incalculable for most of today's material goods), I have proposed the concept and the term "costs per unit of service," abbreviated COPS.

The reason we calculate the costs "per unit of service" is that the function of a product is the service which it fulfills. That is the decisive point. For a car, the COPS would be the price per kilometer, including gasoline and all other costs such as the purchase price, credit costs, insurance, and taxes. Mid-sized cars used for private purposes rarely cost less than 60 euro cents per kilometer (without credit costs), probably more like 70 or 80 euro cents.

For the services we are accustomed to, the price paid by the customer is the same as the COPS. We pay the barber, the taxi driver, or the physician in terms of costs per service unit. In other words, COPS already exists! When you pay your telephone or electricity bill, or buy a train ticket, then you also pay COPS.

This means that service providers are, in principle, paid by COPS. Suppliers of material goods, on the other hand, receive their money for the "costs per item" – and it is left to consumers to find out for themselves how much of the product they need to use in order to get the service they need out of it.

In general, private owners of serviceable products cannot do this. They do not know the COPS, and that means that in the end, they do not know how much they are paying for the utility they are seeking. However, this information could be provided to them, as sketched out using the example of the automobile. One would only need to install instruments similar to taximeters in all motor vehicles that would digitally display the total costs as well as the current costs per kilometer in COPS.

This is how it would work. When a new car is sold, the dealer enters the date and the total costs into the car computer using a check card that comes with the car. The costs include the purchase price as well as those for insurance, taxes, credit, transportation, and registration. The total kilometrage guaranteed by the manufacturer was already logged in the computer before delivery to the dealer. The check card is then always used to pay for filling the tank, maintenance, repairs, tolls, and parking fees, as well as traffic violation tickets. And thanks to a technical connection to the driver's bank, the check card can also be used to register and balance accounts for bank loans, and to pay vehicle taxes and insurance premiums. Without the card, these bills cannot be paid, and the vehicle cannot be started up. Every time the ignition is turned on, the additional amount accrued in the meantime is entered automatically into the car computer. The check card remains with the owner of the vehicle. Of course, it is protected with a personal identification number. When the vehicle is sold, the sale price is entered into the system, and the card is handed over to the new owner.

Integrated in the dashboard, the COPS meter provides up-to-the-minute information about various things: for example, the current costs per kilometer (in euro cents), based on all previous costs and the guaranteed total performance of the car, the monthly costs since the car was purchased, fuel use in cents per kilometer (measured at ten-second intervals), as well as an average value for the current trip, etc.

An automobile dealer could tag a car as follows, taking figures based on experience, fixed costs (such as car taxes), and guaranteed total performance of the vehicle into account:

Price for the car: 31,000 euros
COPS = 70 euros per hundred kilometers (based on normal
    use for a specified number of kilometers guaranteed total
    performance).

We can imagine COPS meters not only for cars, but also for other equipment, machines, or buildings that incur costs during their useful life.

The situation is different for disposable or single-use products (packaging materials, for instance), because no costs arise due to their use. This applies to many objects with long life spans as well, for example sundials, linen chests, paintings, or jewelry. Simple tools and manually used equipment do not incur consequential costs worth mentioning, either, even if some materials – such as a few droplets of oil – are added now and then.

You will have noticed long ago: the only objects that cause consequential costs during their use are those that have built-in motors, heating, cooling, and illumination as well as those that use electricity and require regular maintenance. Costs for disposal, however, may arise for all products.

COPS tells us how much money we actually have to spend to use the service provided by a particular product. Unfortunately, these financial costs have little to do with the so-called "environmental costs," that is, with the amount of "consumption" of nature necessary to make this service available.

In order to get a grip on environmental consumption throughout a product's entire life, I proposed a metric early on, namely MIPS, life-long Material Input (including energy) Per unit of Service for "service delivery machines." In other words, MIPS transcends the concept of the ecological rucksack and ends only when the piece of equipment has been disposed of.

As we have already discussed, the MI in MIPS is given in metric tons, kilograms, or grams. In contrast, the service S is "dimensionless" and must be defined as the specific performance a good offers, as we will see below. What is decisive here is the "basic service." For a car, for example, person-kilometers. Additional desires and special conditions are initially of secondary importance. A car does not need heated leather seats to do what it was invented to do.

For products that use resources during their use, for example washing machines, the MI in MIPS is calculated as the sum of the ecological rucksack, plus the washing machine's own weight, plus the sum of all material inputs (including energy) for a defined service (S). For a washing machine, for instance, "cleaning 5 kilograms of clothing" lends itself as the service.

If we are talking about a product that is used just once (this applies, for example, to a paper cup, but not for a "single-use camera," which is reloaded with fresh film up to thirty times and resold), then S = 1 and MIPS = ecological rucksack plus the product's own weight.

If we are concerned with products with very long life spans – such as sundials, paintings, or chairs – that is, products that provide their services over a very long period of time without resource use, then MIPS = the product's rucksack MI plus the product's own weight, divided by a very large number of units of service S which have been or are yet to be provided. In other words, MIPS is very small for "undemanding" durable products, which means that the resource productivity of such objects can be extremely high. These goods are of particular interest from an ecological point of view.

MIPS can be defined and described in different ways: MIPS = material input per unit of service = ecological total costs (referring to consumption of materials and energy) for using a service unit provided by a "service delivery machine" = ecological costs of use for a product = the subsidy provided by the environment per unit of service.

MIPS is evidently the ecological equivalent of COPS

COPS answers the question: "What am I really getting for my money?"

MIPS permits us to understand: "How high is the environmental subsidy for this service?" Accordingly, future eco-innovations will distinguish themselves by new forms of use and service provision which satisfy needs at least as well as conventional goods and services, but require substantially less resource consumption per unit of service.

In other words, both MIPS and COPS are metrics in the best tradition of economic principles: what counts is realizing a certain result with a minimum of input; and the goal is to achieve maximum use with a particular input (productivity).

MIPS as well as COPS are metrics that make sense only for goods that provide services, in other words, they are not appropriate for raw materials or other materials. A raw material such as coal or a material such as aluminum does not provide a service. Services are provided only by the products and services for which these resources are used. There is no MIPS for coal or aluminum, only for the power plant that burns the coal, for the service "generating electricity" for which coal is burned, and for the window frames that are made of aluminum.

The service unit S

MIPS relates the input of materials and energy (MI) to one or more service units (S) for which this input was calculated. We must agree on the definition of a service unit in order to be able to use MIPS. Service units are units of use which involve having a good at one's disposal (ownership, possession, or right to use). The terms "service" and "use" mean the same thing in this context; they are used synonymously. We differentiate three ways of determining a service unit, depending on the product:

1. The service provided by land motor vehicles – for example, trucks, automobiles, and motorcycles, but not ships or airplanes – whose main purpose is to overcome distances, is measured in kilometers, and we must also take into consideration the amount of freight or number of people transported per kilometer. The calculation of MIPS includes the total of all service units, from beginning-of-use until end-of-use.

2. The service provided by equipment, machinery, and products that have a built-in use cycle, is given for a particular number

of cycles. This applies, for example, to washing machines, dishwashers, clothes dryers, wind-up clocks, flush toilets, cement mixers, and coffee makers. For such products, the total number of service units is counted as well, in this case the number of cycles from the beginning to the end of the product's useful life. In addition, the amount processed per cycle must be given. For instance, a washing machine washes five kilograms of laundry per cycle. That is the service it provides. The total number of its service units is the number of loads of laundry that it can clean. Analogously, a clock can be wound a limited number of times and then runs for a certain duration, and a coffee maker prepares a pot of six or twelve cups of coffee a certain number of times.

3. For equipment, machines, products, and buildings whose duration of use is determined by the users themselves, the duration of use is employed as the service unit, whereby the number of people benefiting from use during this time period or the capacity must also be taken into account. The service provided by a stove, for instance, depends not only on its duration of use, but also on the number of people eating the food cooked on the stove and the number of burners that can be used simultaneously. Other examples: the capacity of a vacuum cleaner is its suction power; the capacity of a computer monitor is the size of the screen; for a building, the capacity is determined by the floor space; and the capacity of a refrigerator is usually given in terms of its volume.

The duration of use can be divided into individual periods of use that last different lengths of time. Whenever possible, the periods of use are determined so that they correspond to the smallest meaningful time span for an individual instance of use. In other words, they are measured:

- in less than one hour, for example for the use of signal transmission devices, brushes for polishing shoes, tools, wristwatches.
- in hours, for instance for the use of airplanes, vacuum cleaners, stoves, light bulbs, roller skates, computers, television sets, and other consumer electronics.
- in days, for cut flowers, for example.
- in years, for goods with a long life span and goods whose use is subject to changing frequency and intensity. Goods with a long life span include, among others, buildings, swimming pools, highway bridges, infrastructures, works of art, road building machinery, heating systems, furniture, boats, bathrooms, dishes, cutlery, and books.

Determining a service unit always also depends on the object of investigation, and in particular, it depends on what is to be compared. When comparing two or more products, the smallest possible common service unit should be defined, for example transporting one person for one kilometer (one person-kilometer). This allows the direct comparison of the input of materials and energy required by different means of transportation (bus, train, automobile) to provide this unit of service.

If one were to ask ten people to rank a number of products according to their utility, they would probably give ten different answers. Whether or not something is useful, and whether it is more useful than the product offered by the competition, is a question of subjective priorities and preferences, among other things. However, since scientific criteria cannot help us to compare different subjective assessments, determining comparable units of service serves as a pragmatic and practical compromise. In the end, of course, it is always a matter of personal decisions. However, it does make a difference whether this decision is supported by comprehensible facts and a clearly defined yardstick such as MIPS, or whether the people making the decision are entirely dependent on their subjective judgment and the prior knowledge they happen to have. For example, few people will have trouble making a decision if they are offered two alternatives for traveling to a particular destination. Nonetheless, it may be valuable to know before making the decision that one mode of travel causes considerably more environmental damage per person-kilometer than the other.

An example: what is dematerialized steel?

A leading German steel industry executive once asked cunningly what he, as an "eco-layperson," should make of the concept of dematerialized steel. Steel was steel, wasn't it, and subtracting material from mass would just mean less of the same steel.

Of course, that isn't what dematerialization is all about. Using less steel does dematerialize a car body made of steel. But a ton of steel is still a ton of steel. One can dematerialize a ton of steel only by starting with the material intensities (MI) beginning at its "cradle," that is, beginning with mining ore. However, even for steel, there is certainly still room for improvement. For example, one can use less water or reduce transports; one can run the blast furnace in a different way or produce (ecologically less costly) electric furnace steel, and one can smelt more scrap metal. In short, one can minimize the ecological rucksack.

When the executive heard this, he promptly began to recite a long list of such improvements, some of them already implemented, others still planned, and asked what that had to do with ecology. At best, they would only save a little bit of carbon dioxide!

That may sound right, but it overlooks the important aspect of MIPS that lies in focusing directly on the utility of products as the crucial factor. For example, bridges can be made of steel. The purpose of a bridge is to provide a way of driving across one side of a valley to the other. This utility – the service – can be achieved in different ways: by a bridge made of concrete, by a bridge made of steel, or by a very long road leading downhill and then uphill.

The ecological rucksack of a bridge made of steel, however, is – in terms of its utility – substantially smaller than that of a bridge made of concrete, let alone the long road, which also devours open space. In the end, the German steel industry executive found this suggestion quite interesting.

Resource productivity: more utility for less environment

The terms "material input" (MI) and MIPS are very closely linked to a term well-known to practitioners in industry: productivity. The smaller the amount of material needed to provide a service, the more productively the resources are used. Unproductive use of natural resources means the same thing as high material input. In mathematical terms, resource productivity and material consumption are inversely proportional to one another; if one is reduced, the other is increased, and vice versa. And just as there is material input (MI) or the ecological rucksack on the one side and material input per unit of service (MIPS) on the other, we must also differentiate between two types of resource productivity. Depending on whether we are concerned with certain products or providing services, we speak of resource productivity of production or resource productivity of the service.

Resource productivity of production is a metric for the efficiency of energy and material input in making a product. The smaller the ecological rucksack (ER) of a product, the larger the resource productivity of its manufacture.

To recapitulate: the ecological rucksack is the amount of material that needs to be "loaded onto the back" of a product to show how large the amount of environmental resources encapsulated in the product is. The mass of the product and the ecological rucksack together make up the total material input (MI) for the product. For this reason, we calculate the resource productivity of production by dividing the weight of the product by the sum of the product's weight and the ecological rucksack, in other words, by the material intensity (MI).

To provide an example, let us use a calculation performed by Christopher Manstein of the Wuppertal Institute. If a motorcycle weighs 190 kilograms (0.19 metric tons) and its ecological rucksack weighs 3.3 metric tons (without the motorcycle's own weight), then resource productivity is calculated as $0.19/(3.3+0.19) = 0.054$. This means that only 5.4% of the (abiotic) raw materials removed from their natural locations were transformed into a machine providing utility – hardly a technical achievement that should fill us with pride.

But as we have seen, this calculation is not complete from an ecological point of view because we need to take into account not only the natural raw materials for manufacturing the motorcycle, but also those needed to use it. Motorcycles do use gasoline, after all, when you ride them, and mousetraps require cheese. As a very rough rule of thumb, the ecological rucksack for the entire lifetime of service-providing machines that consume resources while they are being used is about twice as big as the rucksack for their production alone. For the motorcycle in our example, including use lowers resource productivity to approximately 2.8%.

Unfortunately, this is by no means a particularly extreme example. On average, the machines we produce have an ecological rucksack of thirty metric tons per metric ton of product. By a rough estimate and on average, the entire industry of manufacturers of technical products in Germany attains resource productivity of $1/(30+1)$ or approximately 3.2%.

Resource productivity of services

Up to now, I have not yet spoken of services when discussing resource productivity. I have demonstrated how to calculate the resource productivity of a product, disregarding for now the service the product provides once it has been manufactured. Once resource productivity has been calculated, one can usually determine very quickly where improvements can be made. However, as I mentioned above, I consider the opportunities for dematerializing our economic system to be much greater if we do not use existing products as our starting point, but rather think about which needs for services we have and then seek a way to fulfill those needs in a way which requires the least possible amount of resources.

What we need to improve is the resource productivity of providing services or utility, that is, the resource productivity of the production of a unit of performance or service S, divided by the material input MI, or the product's own weight plus its ecological rucksack.

The resource productivity of the service is calculated as S per MI. We have already examined this the other way around: MI per S is MIPS: material input per unit of service. We see that the resource productivity of the utility of a service-providing machine is the inverse of MIPS. That means MIPS is a measure for the resource productivity of the service.

The resource productivity of services can be improved by means of eco-intelligent innovations in the technical realm; in other words, by reducing material intensity in technically sophisticated ways. But that is not the only way. Increasing the factor utility achieves the same result. Improvements in this sphere are open to each and every human being. If people make conscious decisions to save resources, by doing so, they achieve the same goal as inventors and design engineers with technical innovations: they improve the resource productivity of the service provided by a product. One group, the technicians, reduces MI; the other group, the consumers, increases S, the utility. The participation of the consumers in this process of improvement is enormously important: after all, a consumer's decision in favor of the solution with the smaller amount of resource consumption can improve productivity on a scale which technicians would need decades to achieve with new inventions, if they could indeed achieve it at all. Changing consumer behavior is often the most rapid way to drastic improvements of resource productivity. Let us call it, for short, a "private" increase in the resource productivity of services.

For example, anyone can carpool with colleagues instead of each person using a car of his or her own. If two people ride in the same car, rather than in two cars as before, then the car they use provides its service with twice the previous resource productivity – from one day to the next. That is a spectacular improvement; from a technical point of view, a century's leap in efficiency. Since the beginning of the industrial revolution, technical improvements in the efficiency of existing systems of about 0.5 % per year have been the rule.

A similar effect can be attained by a family that decides to use a carsharing or carpooling arrangement with other families or to use the family car for a longer period of time before buying a new one. One can also reuse aluminum foil in the kitchen several times or rent sports equipment that is rarely used rather than buying it. The variety of possibilities is substantially larger than the technical potential that exists even when employing the most sophisticated technology.

In all cases, it is of decisive importance that the improvement of a service's resource productivity based on a personal decision does not require any technical changes, that it works immediately, and that it always saves money.

The higher the prices of the natural raw materials employed to manufacture a product, the more it pays to improve the "technical" resource productivity of manufacturing. If, for example, one were to manufacture certain parts of a piece of technical equipment out of gold, then it would be worth designing these parts to be as small as possible, or seeking cheaper alternative materials. (This is one of the very great opportunities for chemical industry.) At the moment, however, most natural raw materials are relatively cheap: for the price of two packs of cigarettes, one can buy a metric ton of sand or two metric tons of drinking water, delivered through the faucet in your kitchen. Small wonder, then, that only a few business people so far have been pointedly using this path to improve their profits. It requires innovative intelligence, tenacity, and long-term planning.

"Ecological prices" and labels

In a television show about our work on the MIPS concept, the host wanted to illustrate vividly for viewers what it would mean for them if MIPS were one day used to valuate products. His short film was set in a department store. The camera panned along the shelves and the products, which displayed the familiar price tags. But the tags also had information about how much MIPS had to be assigned to the product. The audience could see: if two competing products have roughly the same price, then of course one would buy the one with the smaller material intensity per service unit provided. And if consumers wanted to make environmentally-friendly purchasing decisions, then they might be willing to pay a little more for the ecologically 'better' product.

In his film, the journalist had realized what I had indeed been hoping for: labeling products and services so that consumers can see the price the environment is "paying" for them to be able to purchase this service or that product. In real life, I would expect that the consumer would prefer a low price over a low MIPS purchase in most cases.

Let us take a look at how such "ecological prices" in the currency of MIPS could be determined in practice. Fundamentally, an ecological price must be a comprehensible metric for the extent to which the product or the service is a burden on the environment. Ecological prices must express in physical units the potential of material goods and services to place strain on the environment; in other words, ecological potentials for disturbances. Inasmuch as the environmental stress is a result of resource consumption, these prices can be equated with the ecological rucksacks of materials and of material goods that provide services.

Why shouldn't the price tag of the future include information about ecological rucksacks in euros and cents or the currency of the country, in addition to the price itself as a matter of course, with the ecological information calculated "from the cradle to the retailer" or, better yet, in MIPS?

The exciting question is whether and to what extent such

labeling could contribute to furthering our economy on the path towards sustainability. We know that information about the absence of environmental toxins in foods influences consumers' decision-making considerably. If, for instance, a manufacturer guarantees that his products are free of intentionally applied herbicides and pesticides, then he can sell these products at considerably higher prices. However, this purchasing behavior certainly also has a lot to do with consumers' desire for personal health – probably substantially more than it has to do with their general concern for the state of the environment.

From the perspective of environmental protection, it would be more interesting to know whether, for example, apples from New Zealand are less popular with consumers than apples from the Lake Constance region or from Merano. Studies about the effectiveness of information on a product's country of origin are better suited to investigating whether and how concern for the environment influences consumer behavior. Do customers prefer oranges from Israel to oranges from Spain? The difference in the monetary price is minimal. For all intents and purposes, the considerable open and hidden subsidies for transportation in Europe (and other regions of the world) conceal the differences between distances entirely.

Labeling products using the units of ecological rucksack or MIPS alone would not help consumers much in making their purchasing decisions. What does ER (Ecological Rucksack) = 255 mean, after all? Is that a lot? Or a little? Can I afford it? Consumers can directly relate every single monetary price to their personal budgets and their economic interests. A price of 2.50 euros for a small plastic toy may seem expensive, but it is not a major cost factor. A price of 250,000 euros for a condominium in a good location may be cheap, but if this sum exceeds the buyer's budget, then the condo will be too expensive after all.

But: what is the budget for comparison with the ecological rucksack? The consumer cannot relate an "environmental destruction potential" expressed in ecological rucksacks or MIPS to the overall health of the environment.

Even though labeling goods with an ecological price tag alone is unlikely to result in decisive progress towards sustainability, it seems to me that the development of an eco-label for industrial goods which can be generally applied and harmonized on an international level, is nonetheless sensible and important, for several reasons:

Firstly, well-to-do groups of consumers in Germany actually do take ecological labeling into account insofar as they trust the label. Manufacturers tend to be well-informed about consumers' purchasing behavior and respond accordingly. So labeling could also provide a bit of a push towards sustainability.

Early trials with children have shown that, secondly, it is indeed possible to give young people a good understanding of the relevance of ecological rucksacks even at an early age, and within a short period of time. The purpose of the Wuppertal Institute's project "MIPS for Kids," headed by Maria Welfens and Heike Steinkamp, is to show additional ways to teach children and young people about the MIPS concept. Disseminating this knowledge broadly throughout the field of education would be desirable to make consumers familiar with the economic and ecological meaning of resource productivity as early as possible. Regardless of the extent to which it will be possible to integrate values expressing "environmental interference" or COPS in the purchase price of products or services in the future, knowledge of ecological rucksacks and MIPS will be needed not least to determine tariffs, and also to monitor the hopefully narrowing gap between today's prices that are "not telling the 'ecological truth'" (Ernst Ulrich von Weizsäcker) and a more realistic price structure in the future.

Ecological prices

I have defined the ecological rucksack so that it includes all natural raw materials used, from the cradle to the final material or product, minus the product's own weight. The ecological rucksack (ER) plus the product's own weight is the material input (MI). As we have already seen, we can differentiate five rucksacks: one each for abiotic and biotic natural raw materials, one for water, one for air, and finally, one for movements of earth. Although rucksacks for water (for instance, for processing ore) and air (for example, for transportation) also arise during the production of abiotic materials such as nickel, electric steel, and copper on the path from the source to the material, for the sake of simplicity, I have opted to take only the abiotic rucksacks into account when estimating the ecological prices of abiotic materials.

Therefore, to determine the ecological price of materials, we need only provide the mass of natural materials which must be moved per metric ton of material, plus that of energy, until the material can be used in a technical process. Price tags for abiotic materials could look something like this in the future:

Sand (metric ton):   €10 MI 1.2 (metric tons/metric ton)
Nickel (metric ton):   €11,200 MI 141 (metric tons/metric ton)
Electric steel (metric ton): €620 MI 3.36 (metric tons/metric ton)
Copper (metric ton):   €3250 MI 500 (metric tons/metric ton)
Gold (metric ton): €22,600,000 MI 540,000 (metric tons/metric ton)

Let us now take a look at the ecological prices of material goods that can provide service or utility. If we take the material input as the ecological price, then a price tag for a three-way catalytic converter, for example, could look like this: three-way catalytic converter: 1200 euros; MI 2.7 (metric tons per unit). And for a gold ring: ring (gold, seven grams): 550 euros; MI 3.8 (metric tons per ring).

We could even determine the ecological price for a painting by Rembrandt in this way. Let us assume that the painting weighs ten kilograms (without the frame), has an (assumed) ecological rucksack of 100 (the pigments also contain heavy metals) and an estimated market value of twenty million euros. The result:

Painting (Rembrandt): 20,000,000 euros; MI 0.1 (metric tons per painting). In other words; investing in works of art can be exceptionally rewarding from an ecological point of view.

Let us take a look at a few more examples, everyday objects we can all imagine buying:

Nail (steel):	€0.01	MI 0.0000036 (metric tons per nail)
Nail (copper):	€0.05	MI 0.0004 (metric tons per nail)
Automobile (mid-range model):	€30,000	MI 45 (metric tons per automobile)
Automobile (luxury model):	€90,000	MI 70 (metric tons per automobile)

In order to obtain this result, one must take into account that a luxury car will drive about twice as many miles during its life span as a mid-range car. So we have to compare two mid-range cars with one luxury model: let us assume the luxury model will do a total of approximately 400,000 kilometers in its life span, and a mid-range car only 200,000. From the 'cradle' to the dealership, two mid-range cars 'cost' ninety metric tons, and a luxury model 'costs' seventy metric tons.

Next, let us consider the ecological prices of services, MIPS.

The mid-range car needs approximately seven liters of fuel per 100 kilometers, the luxury model, on the other hand, requires eleven liters. Mid-range cars will then use about 4000 times seven liters for 400,000 kilometers, or twenty-eight metric tons of fuel. Since the material input factor MIF of fuel is about 1.2, the ecological price for this fuel is thirty-four metric tons. The same calculation for the luxury car gives us a result of fifty-three metric tons (4000 times 11 times 1.2). All in all, the material inputs of mid-range cars over a distance of 400,000 kilometers add up to 118 metric tons; the corresponding figure for luxury cars is 123 metric tons (excluding tires, repairs, infrastructures, etc.).

This is merely a rough initial comparison. In both cases, the consumption of nature makes up approximately 300 grams of (non-renewable) nature per kilometer, without taking MI for tires, oil, etc., as well as the infrastructure for road traffic into consideration. According to the newest research results from Finland, the ecological infrastructure costs per kilometer driven by a car can be up to ten (!) times higher than the ecological costs of the vehicle itself.

Let us finally turn briefly to the ecological prices of foods. Strictly speaking, we must pack so much into the ecological rucksacks of foods that the calculation is very complex. For this reason, I will limit this example to the ecological price "from the cradle to the sale by the producer." In other words, I will disregard seed production, chemicals, transportation, processing, keeping the food fresh, and packaging on the way to the consumer.

From the perspective of resource productivity, one can express the ecological price of foods most simply by using erosion as an indicator. We will focus on that part of erosion which can definitely be ascribed to food production, and will pack the proportion of erosion into each food's rucksack which is related to that particular food. The result is a figure in metric tons of erosion per metric ton of food produced. S. Bringezu and H. Schütz at the Wuppertal Institute calculated the erosion intensity for the biomasses imported into Germany. The values for domestically grown products of agriculture and forestry are very similar. The values fluctuate considerably and point towards three important insights:

1. All of today's production of biomass by agriculture and forestry is remarkably resource-intensive, measured in metric tons of erosion per metric ton of product, and can indeed be compared with the resource consumption by industrial products in metric tons per metric ton from the cradle to the product (we already mentioned the high proportion of waste in biomass production).

2. Veal and beef have rates of erosion in the exporting countries that are comparable to the biotic material input factor (MIF) for the meat of these animals. That is, not only is the resource efficiency of animal protein production very low regarding resource input per unit of output, it is also cut in half by the erosion it causes.

3. Present-day cultivation methods for the production of biodiesel in particular, as well as other renewable energy sources, carry ecological rucksacks far greater than the MIF values of fuels from fossil energy sources. Proposals to switch from fossil fuels to biofuels extracted from crops should therefore be reviewed with care, and life-cycle-wide calculations should be performed before decisions are made.

These insights should generally be taken into account when discussing and making decisions about putting renewable resources to industrial use, whether as materials or as sources of energy.

Furthermore, it is recommended that price tags on fruit and other foods should include the region where it was grown (oranges from Florida, apples from New Zealand, ham from northern Germany). Stating the country of origin is already a legal requirement in the EU, but it would make sense to require additional information about the region of origin within larger countries, for instance the UK or Germany, for staples that can be grown almost everywhere. On the other hand, the country of origin of the biomass used as feed should be given for meat and fish (soy from Brazil, fish meal from Japan), as it causes the largest amount of transportation and therefore the highest ecological costs.

Do prices tell the ecological truth?

For years, one of the most notable statements by Ernst Ulrich von Weizsäcker has been that prices do not tell the ecological truth. Many products and raw materials are available at prices that do not reflect in the slightest the extent of the interference in the ecosphere necessary for providing them. Nobody is apt to doubt that this statement is correct. If we content ourselves with using ecological rucksacks to estimate the potential of material goods for ecological disturbance, we can indeed compare different goods with each other and arrive at statements about "the ecological untruth" of their market prices.

To do so, we examine for a number of materials how many metric tons the material input per metric ton of material weighs. In other words, we calculate the material input in metric tons per metric ton (t/t). We compare the result with the price per metric ton by dividing the ecological rucksack by the price. (World market prices for materials change on a daily basis. The prices used here may diverge substantially from the current rate. However, this is irrelevant for our comparison.)

According to Table 3, when we purchase electric steel, we get a relatively small amount of ecological rucksack per euro; in other words: the ecological rucksack of electric steel is to be had at a relatively high price. Seen from this perspective, on the other hand, copper is ecologically speaking cheaper than sand, and gold is more than four times cheaper than electric steel. One can also say that the prices of these materials differ from the "ecological truth" and from each other by a factor of twenty-eight. The prices would be "ecologically true" if the material input cost about the same per metric ton, regardless of the product.

Material	MI (abiotic)/euro
Copper	0.308
Sand	0.2
Gold	0.0480
Nickel	0.0252
Electric steel	0.01096

Table 2 Comparison of material input and price of abiotic materials

But this is not true even for products as similar to each other as the different fossil energy carriers. Here, the prices vary by a factor of twenty-four from one another and from the "ecological truth" by a factor of twenty-four, as our calculations at the Wuppertal Institute have shown for some time already (Table 3).

If we compare the ratio of material input and price for some serviceable material goods, we see that the price of the Rembrandt painting is 450,000 times as ecologically beneficial ('more true') than the price of the three-way catalytic converter, about five million times as ecologically favorable as the price of gold, and thirty million times as ecologically beneficial as the price of copper. It is not entirely surprising that works of art are among the goods to be recommended in ecological terms, at least as

Energy carrier	MI/euro abiotic	MI/euro standardized
Lignite	0.112	21
Coal (imported)	0.132	24
Heating oil	0.024	4.4
Coal (domestic German)	0.0188	4.1
Diesel	0.0054	1
Light heating oil	0.0104	2.1
Natural gas	0.0072	1.3

Table 3 Comparison of material input (MI) and price of some energy
carriers. Index: diesel = 1

long as they are not monumental works, unless they were created
from recycled parts or materials.

Apparently, Ernst Ulrich von Weizsäcker's comment about
the "ecological untruth" of prices is correct. In order to advance
towards both truth and a dematerialized economy, we recom-
mend labeling products with a measure such as MIPS. This ecological measure provides consumers with a universally applicable
tool to compare products according to their ecological quality
and enables them to make eco-intelligent purchasing decisions.

Neither economic survival nor biological existence is possible on planet Earth without material flows caused by economic activity and use of land area. Economy and ecology, the economic system and the environment – for better or for worse, these two complex non-linear systems are interwoven with one another. Constant exchange takes place between them, with material and energy flowing and land use changing between the spheres. This link is inevitable, and an economic system which keeps a distance from nature and does not touch upon the environment, in other words, which is "environmentally friendly," does not exist and cannot exist (Fig. 8).

When we want to manufacture clothing, housing or means of transportation, we must draw on resources provided by nature. We cannot refrain from interfering in the environment. We come from nature and make use of it. We only have the option firstly to understand and accept the close linkage between the economic system and the ecosphere and secondly to take this insight into account throughout the entire economy in a deliberate and planned way. We can only create room to maneuver by ensuring that the services which the ecosphere provides for us, and which we depend upon existentially, can still be provided after our interference and are still available for future generations.

In principle, it would be desirable to attain a state between the two above-mentioned complex systems that one could call

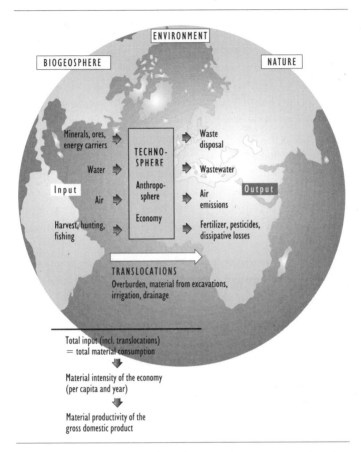

Figure 8 We remove resources from the natural environment (air, soil, water, minerals, living matter) to make the goods and food we need

After they have served their purpose, they are returned to nature ("to the cradle"), whereby the materials originally lifted from the earth have all been altered. Material flow accounts record all components for defined economic areas, including imports from and exports to other countries, and assemble them like a puzzle to get the big picture.

"co-evolution." This expression is to denote a situation in which both the economic and the ecological can develop further – each realm both by itself and in close contact with the other. Evolutionary changes are inevitable in both spheres, practically as if it were a law of nature, as can easily be made clear.

As to the economy, on the one hand, it constantly requires new ideas for innovative and competitive products and services which it uses to create improvements in quality of life and security for a growing number of people. Continuing progress and development of this kind can only work, however, if we can keep on extracting the necessary resources from the ecosphere in the future as well. If the environment no longer provides us with them, if it withholds the services that go along with the resources, then the economy and the food supply will collapse.

Regarding the ecosphere, it is constantly evolving by adapting to changing conditions, following its own laws and at its own speed. But it will not be able to continue to do so in its own way if an all-too-greedy economic system plans in an all-too-short-term and shortsighted way and treats nature as a seemingly inexhaustible stock of provisions which is to be exploited as quickly and as efficiently as possible and turned into products and returns on investment.

This can also be illustrated as follows: there should be a symbiosis, a biocoenosis that benefits all those involved, between the human social environment, the technosphere, and the natural environment. The nature of a symbiosis lies in the partners' behavior adapting in such a way that the benefits gained remain, thereby improving the probability of survival.

In the realms of business and policy, there are still decision-makers who consider material growth to be an important condition for the healthy development of the economy, as a model that has been successful in recent centuries. And in this context, it is very easy for them to hold the opinion that fundamentally, no physical limits on the amount of material exchange between the economy and the ecosphere exist. Based on this premise, they do not give the material metabolism particular relevance regarding the scientific understanding of economic processes. According to this way of thinking, the "environmental problem" is not a difficulty inherent to the system, but rather the inconvenient sum of "external" matters. This refers to the perceptible and measurable damages to the environment and health that the economic activities of certain actors visibly and demonstrably inflict on the environment and human beings. This is the case, for example, when industrial lead emissions cause disease in people who live nearby, or when the level of contaminants in trees in the vicinity of copper smelters increases and the forest begins to die.

Such observations helped raise people's awareness about the environment in the early 1970s; in order to improve the situation, pioneers in this regard developed the concept of the "polluter pays principle," according to which the party responsible for causing damage to others and to their property is liable for the cost of the damage. This idea, while immediately plausible, could not be implemented readily in political and legal terms, and was soon expanded to the effect that the potential polluter should attempt to avoid any environmental damage from occurring in the first place, which was to be achieved by using appropriate means of environmental technology early on. Of course it costs money to develop and use such techniques, and as businesses have no choice in the final analysis but to pass on additional costs due to government regulation to their customers, it is not difficult to foresee that therefore, the prices of goods and services will rise accordingly.

This view is based on the conviction that environmental damages could be limited, avoided, and – if necessary – repaired, thereby making them disappear if appropriate technical means were employed. It is perfectly clear that such strategies result in additional costs, both for the polluters themselves – if it is possible to identify them – and for the regulating authorities. Experience has shown that this type of environmental protection involves political turbulence in addition to financial burdens, since all of the measures decided on by individual countries must be harmonized among the Member States of the European Union and with other trading partners in order to avoid unfair competition.

The proposition, voiced frequently in this context, that appropriate economic growth makes it possible to bear such costs still seems to be widespread today. According to the established methods of calculation employed by our economic advisors, the expenses for such measures to protect and repair the environment also contribute to increasing gross domestic product (GDP), the basic economic metric for all "progress." In this way, end-of-pipe environmental protection as just described even helps boost economic growth.

Economic experts who do not recognize the causal relationship between the ability of ecological services to function on the one hand and the material exchange between the economy and the ecosphere on the other will not be inclined to pay much attention to the natural limits to growth, globalization, trade, and the acquisition of assets. To them, limitless physical growth of the world's economy must be desirable and possible.

An Excursus: *The Tower Of Babel*

Wouter van Dieren has a wonderful story to tell about unlimited material growth: Pieter Bruegel the Elder (c. 1525–1569) painted a picture of the tower of Babel as he saw it in his mind's eye, following the report in Genesis 11:1–9 in the Old Testament.

The story of the tower begins approximately 3500 years ago in Babylon with the wish on the part of the omnipotent ruler of lower Mesopotamia to become near to God, to be his equal as closely as possible. His way of doing so was to use nature's resources to build an immensely high tower. The wisest priests, architects, and engineers of the empire were called together. The best economic experts estimated the costs. They meticulously worked out a simple method for tracking progress on the venture. In order to be fore-armed against collapses, and also to be able to spiral upwards with the necessary transports, the structure obviously had to be shaped like a pyramid, or better like a cone. Its base had to be gigantic so that it could be built high enough.

Construction began with noisy blaring of trumpets. Thousands of poor peasants were drafted to work on the tower. The overseers and the managers of the transport trade, the brickworks, and the region's forests soon became rich and powerful beyond measure. Following the wishes of the economic experts, a monitoring station was established at the entrance of the future pyramid to determine the numbers of workers and transports going up and down, enabling them to communicate daily to the king the good tidings of how his dream was growing. The project's fame grew far beyond the empire's borders. More and more people came from faraway countries to join in the ascent to heaven. The time came that workers and their masters as well as animals had to be housed and fed within the construction site because it had become too far to go up and down every day. Innovations were urgently needed, and human labor was replaced by intelligent tools and machinery to absorb the growing labor costs. Houses, kitchens, roads, stores, and infirmaries were established one after the other at ever higher levels.

Figure 9 *The Tower of Babel* by Pieter Bruegel

The numbers of construction workers, facilities on and inside the tower, and the movements at the pyramid's entrance increased constantly. The confusion of languages on this multinational undertaking grew more severe: the signals to the construction workers and managers became ever more unintelligible and prone to misunderstanding, and communication more and more troublesome. The distances to the sources of building materials and the workers' provisions grew longer and longer. Some even began to spread rumours about a kind of globalization. These necessities, too, were considered part of the entire project's growth and were proudly announced to the ruler every day.

Over time, the downward movements of garbage and corpses increased more and more, the upward movements of construction materials for the expansion of the tower were crowded out by loads for maintenance, repairs, and provisions. Unwavering, the monitoring station at the entrance to the ramp continued to announce growth. Gradually, the confusion of languages and commands became overpowering. The decay of the edifice prevailed. And finally, new construction was stopped entirely. The project of limitless growth had ended. The economic flight of fancy disappeared in the mists of history. Only tales handed down at the bedouins' campfires endured for millennia.

Did this story give you the impression that there is nothing new under the sun, too? In any case, there seem to be astounding similarities between the tower of Babel and our present-day situation.

Inseparable: economic activity and the ecosphere

Sustainable consumption and the management of natural resources in the entire economy go far beyond the question of how we deal sustainably with individual resources and their use, such as forests, oil reserves, soils, or fish stocks. Rather, the issue is how to make the physical foundation of man's economic

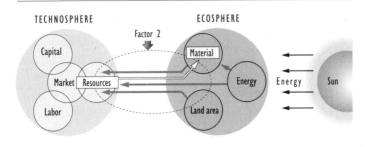

Figure 10   The symbiosis between the ecosphere and the economy

The economy of the man-made technosphere removes natural resources from the ecosphere: material and land area. Capital, labor, and resources – the three ingredients for production – are shown in the technosphere. Today, the economy still derives most of its energy from fossil energy carriers. In the future, the energy needs of the economy must be covered by harvesting solar and geothermal energy by dematerialized technology, that is, it must be ecologically "neutralized" as far as possible. Material that has become useless is transferred back to the ecosphere ("to the cradle"). In order to approach sustainability, the global consumption of material resources has to be cut in half.

activity sustainable by restructuring the consumption of nature in the entire realm of production and consumption.

From a scientific point of view, there is no longer any doubt that the systemic root cause of our environmental problems lies in the inappropriate course of the metabolism between the prosperity-generating machinery of the economy on the one hand and the ecosphere on the other. Therefore, the issue touches on the future viability of the economy itself in a pivotal way, as we can easily see if we look at the big picture. If all of mankind wanted to live according to western patterns of consumption, then one planet Earth would not be sufficient. In addition, the dynamic equilibriums in the atmosphere and the biosphere which were long believed to be stable are displaying changes that are inducing enormous consequential costs for the economy even today.

Day by day, it is becoming ever more apparent how material flows – set in motion by technical means and altered by industrial processes – can change global ecological equilibriums and, as a consequence, can annihilate life and wipe out man-made objects of value. The "once-in-a-century floods," many cyclones and hurricanes, the retreat of glaciers, which has become impossible to overlook, and demonstrably rising sea levels have become part of daily news reporting, which is also speculating about the increasing probability that the Gulf Stream could reverse – with severe consequences for the climate in Europe.

Preserving a "healthy" environment (one that provides the services we need) and the future sustainability of the entire economy are inextricably linked with one another. And since, in the free world, only a productive and just economic system can secure social peace, all three dimensions of sustainability are coupled to resource consumption. For example, it is impossible to create new jobs by means of increased consumption or economic growth as long as goods and services display the resource productivity prevailing today.

Material flow accounts

Material flow accounts can be prepared not only for businesses, but also for private households, regions, countries, and the entire global economy. To begin with, these accounts provide information about how a defined entity of the economy, how a region, a country, or the world, handles the resources extracted from the environment. What is the ratio of the raw materials actually used and the movements of substances such as overburden which fill the ecological rucksacks without providing utility? How much material actually finds its way into the economic system and remains there, and how much is discarded after a short period of time? If we set the results of the balances in relation to the population, we get an indicator we can use to compare the ecological productivity of different regions and countries with one another. Initial data for Germany and other countries is now available. It already shows clearly: the relationship of material throughput and prosperity is by no means in balance. The fact that seventy metric tons of raw materials per year must be moved for every German, but only half that amount for every Japanese (calculated without water in both cases) cannot be explained by differences in the two countries' levels of prosperity, but rather in how generous they are in their use of natural resources.

The resource strategy

Moving, extracting, and changing natural resources for the purpose of creating prosperity leads to a loss of security for life and health as well as to the demolishing of economic goods in an indirect fashion, namely by changing the natural equilibriums of the ecosphere.

Never before in the history of mankind was a material cycle set in motion that could match the one existent today. The metabolism between the economy and the ecosphere has apparently crossed a decisive limit by now. Fifteen years ago, I estimated roughly that 50% less resource extraction worldwide would be necessary. At the time, I was director of the "Material Flows and Research Management" department of the Wuppertal Institute, which was headed by its Founding President Ernst U. von Weizsäcker. This is where the so-called Factor 10 strategy was developed whose goal it was to increase the resource efficiency of industrialized countries by at least a factor of ten on average in the coming decades.

That was the time when my team elaborated the many details necessary for providing the foundation for practical implementation of the central goal of dematerialization by a factor of ten, whereby the economic system was not defined via the sale of products but focused instead on the services provided by these goods.

A new strategy was required because people had realized that the old form of environmental protection – despite all its successes – would not be able to prevent the economy from moving further away from the goal of sustainability. For this reason alone, a new eco-strategy must follow a different formula, for example, the envisaged service economy which, one could hope, could reach the goal of reducing the excessive consumption of resources.

Sustainability policy requires dealing with resource protection at the input side of economic cycles – not just at the end, when the economy and consumers have to pay the consequential costs of non-sustainable development. Resource consumption cannot be regulated by means of government funding, imperatives, or bans, unless one strives to repeat the mistakes of real socialism.

As already suggested, the advantage of a resource strategy lies precisely in the fact that one can use economic policy instruments to create incentives for eco-intelligent market behavior on the part of manufacturers, retailers, and consumers, and above all, by a price increase for natural resources before they are set on their path through the economy. However, such a price rise must be installed in a manner that is cost-neutral for the economy, otherwise it will turn out to be a mammoth eco-tax and will kill the goose that lays the golden egg for us. How this can be done while creating many new jobs at the same time will be discussed below.

When one increases the price of resources, wasting resources is punishment in itself without outside interference, and at all stages of manufacturing, retailing, transportation, storage, and consumption. In addition, wastes finally become what the German Waste Management Act already called them semantically years ago; they turn into "*Wertstoffe*," "materials of value." But the decisive response of the manufacturing sector to increasing resource prices will be to launch products and services with growing resource productivity, that is, with decreasing MIPS. For a considerable part of market competition will then shift to this area.

Material flows in Germany

Since the early 1990s, Stefan Bringezu and Helmut Schütz at the Wuppertal Institute have been grappling intensively with the question of what the physical foundation of Germany's economy really looks like, and in the meantime, they have found friends in many other countries who have compiled comparable data according to the pattern developed in Wuppertal.

No economic system can be based on a self-sufficient foundation of resources today. Gigantic material flows cross all national borders in the form of raw materials as well as manufactured goods. All these material things carry bigger or smaller rucksacks with them, transcending all borders.

If the further development of all economic areas is to be designed in such a manner that the physical processes of exchange between the economy and nature conform to the ecological limits determined by nature, then it is practically essential to identify reliable data about the national and regional material and energy flows first, and in a following step to analyze the distribution of the flows within the nation's economic sectors. Only on the basis of this information will it both make ecological sense and be responsible regarding economic policy to undertake demate-rialization in a targeted fashion in the future.

Let us begin with Germany's material flow balance. The following Fig. 12 shows the situation in 1991.

For the imports of abiotic raw materials, totaling almost 2200 billion metric tons, the ratio of 'unused' materials (= ecological rucksacks) to actually utilized amounts of material is roughly two to one, which means that approximately 66% of these amounts remain in other countries. The ratio of unused to uti-lized amounts is similar for raw materials sourced domestically (disregarding water and air).

The imports of biotic raw materials involved soil erosion of agricultural land abroad five times as high as the amounts cur-rently imported. In total, less than 200 billion metric tons of biotic raw materials were part of Germany's metabolism, that is, significantly less than 5%. When deliberating a reorganization of Germany's raw material base towards renewables, one should first take note of this reality.

The total amount of recycled material is relatively insignifi-cant as well. Even if the figure has doubled since 1991, when it was 64 billion metric tons, this still makes up significantly less than 3 percent of the abiotic (non-renewable) turnover of mate-rial. Figure 13 also clearly shows that theoretically, a maximum of 35% of Germany's material abiotic metabolism can be recycled.

The German economy, like any other, involves materials on a global basis, which means that a significant amount of environ-mental pressure occurs in other countries. Obviously, we cannot exclude these transnational environmental burdens when we con-sider dematerialization at the national level. Otherwise, it might easily happen that domestic improvements are based on creating

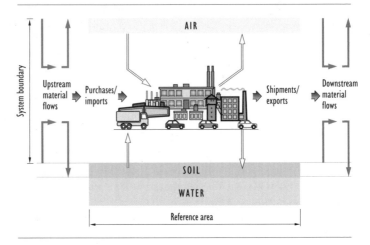

Figure 11   Basic diagram for the analysis of material flows of an
economy (reference area)

The material flow account of the reference area encompasses the entire
exchange of materials ("from the cradle to the grave") with the natural
environment (shown above and below the system boundaries in the diagram)
and with external economic areas. The ecological rucksacks of the upstream
material flows are taken into account when computing the import of resources
into the reference area.

material flows in other countries and regions. For example, France
shifted quarrying of bauxite (the name bauxite has its root in
Les Baux de Provence), from which aluminum is made, to other
countries, which benefited Provence, but was not in the interest of making the world's economy ecologically sustainable. If
Germany were to increase its imports of electricity generated by
coal in the future, then the domestic material flow balance would
look better. But from an ecological point of view, the result would
be a worsening of the situation, for example if the technical efficiency of generating electricity from coal were lower abroad than
in Germany, or if the ecological rucksack were heavier.

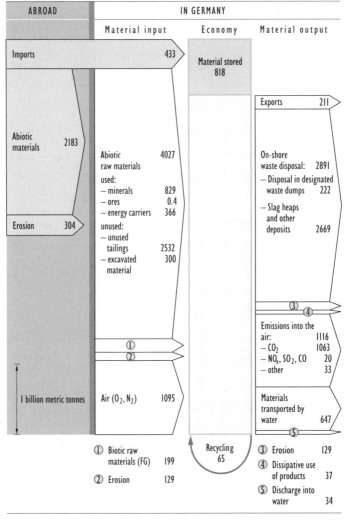

Figure 12 Material flow account for Germany (excluding the use of water) for 1991 in million metric tons, including imports and their rucksacks

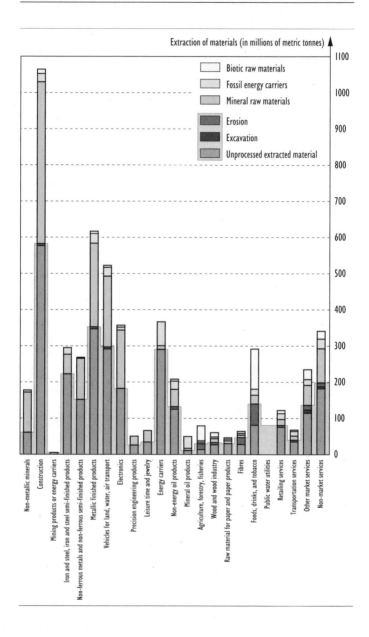

Extraction of materials (in millions of metric tonnes)

Data regarding "transboundary" environmental burdens would surely also be interesting if computed on the basis of smaller geographical areas, for example federal states, districts, counties, and municipalities. For instance, we can be sure that the electricity exports of the German federal state of North Rhine-Westphalia cause significant environmental pressures in that state.

The differences in resource consumption by the various sectors of the German economy are quite significant. Figure 12 shows the results of work by Ralf Behrensmeier and Stefan Bringezu.

We classified the economic sectors following the official statistics of the Federal Republic of Germany. The 'construction and housing' sector tops the list by a wide margin, at approximately twenty metric tons per capita per year. For this reason, it is no accident that we are pursuing architecture and design projects concerned with dematerializing buildings. Examples include the MIPS Institute building in Wuppertal, the Factor 10 building in Lower Austria (rw@grat.at), or the Design Centre (Formens Hus) in Haellefors, Sweden, covering 3000 square meters, which was inaugurated by the Swedish prime minister in November 2005 (www.formenshus.se).

In any case, construction and housing deserve particular attention if Germany is to approach sustainability by reducing material inputs in the economy. Ironically, just the opposite is happening. In the new federal states of former East Germany, public funding promoted the building boom after reunification of the country to such an extent that several years later, approximately one million apartments were vacant. The construction industry then demanded that demolishing housing was to be subsidized in order to provide job security in the industry. Nobody seemed

Figure 13 The resource needs of different economic sectors in Germany

to object to this most curious, even ludicrous idea – neither for economic nor for ecological reasons.

Only today, after unprecedented urban sprawl has altered the appearance of Germany's landscape for decades to come, promoted by governmental support for building single-family homes and for the commute to them through tax relief for kilometers driven as well as publicly financed roads, only after governments have piled up unprecedented debts, has the task of eliminating these economic and ecological absurdities been taken on in earnest.

Food metabolism in Germany

At the end of the last century, the material throughput for providing Germany with food was approximately 350 million metric tons per year, not counting water. That is almost four times less than in the construction material sector. On the input side of the food metabolism, we count the 38 million metric tons of imports, the 176 million metric tons of biomass (including cattle fodder) harvested in Germany, the 129 million metric tons of erosion linked to the cultivation of agricultural land, and the 26 million metric tons of oxygen from the air required for the respiration of food and fodder. The input of non-renewable resources is relatively small. At approximately one million metric tons per year, the fraction of recycled material is practically negligible.

The following measures regarding sustainable development in this sector should be considered:

–   Reducing and preventing erosion domestically. Modern agricultural practices and methods, even cultivating the earth without using plows, can limit the loss of soils. The government should consider offering financial incentives for a limited period of time to better avoid erosion. The consequential costs of erosion at the global level are estimated at roughly 1,200 billion euros (see Meyers and Kent).

— More efficient use of the biomass produced for food. In particular reducing meat consumption in favor of a vegetarian diet would be a sensible option. In addition, the wastes from production and consumption of foods which are currently not being used or reused can be limited, for instance by using them as fodder for pigs, ducks, and chickens, as well as by producing technically useful products (for example, using straw as insulation material, as in the Factor 10 house near St. Pölten in Lower Austria, cf. Schmidt-Bleek (ed.): *Der ökologische Rucksack*).

— Increasing return of nutrient-rich residuals (e.g. sewage sludge) onto agricultural land.

— Raising import levies on erosion and water intensive products (possibly involving paying out the revenue raised to the producing countries under the condition that they introduce measures limiting water consumption and erosion).

— Reviewing the structure and composition of subsidies for agriculture with the goal of increasing material efficiency of the sector and its products. In the year 2000, the agricultural subsidies in the OECD countries totaled almost 300 billion euros per year (while at the same time, the agricultural development measures in the Third World were estimated at a little more than 30 billion euros).

— Reviewing the transportation costs regarding open and hidden subsidies with the goal of approaching the real costs for transporting food (and industrial goods). This could limit the frequently described multiple transports of foods criss-crossing Europe during the different phases of their production. Readers will likely remember Stefanie Boege's infamous tub of yogurt with its requirement of no less than 3500 kilometers to bring its ingredients to one place. In 2000, the subsidies for road transports in OECD countries totaled almost 900 million euros, approximately 60% of which accrued in the United States.

Foods in the form in which they arrive on the consumers' plate via the market, as well as their preparation for consumption, are no longer imaginable without the use of many technologies. This applies to all foods, with the exception of a minuscule amount, namely those directly gathered or hunted in the ecosphere, such as mushrooms, berries, or wild boar. But in contrast to Obelix's day, today even wild boar are brought down, carved, skinned, frozen, dried, and transported employing elaborate technology.

Material flows in the European Union

If we desire to evaluate the potentials for environmental pressures emerging as a result of material flows, and if we aim to draw conclusions for the dematerialization of the economy from this, then the development of the trend of material consumption plays a major role. Figure 14 shows important trends of material consumption in the EU-15 since 1980. The TMF (Total Material Flow) has not changed significantly during this period of time, in other words, the material input per monetary unit of turnover has been decoupled significantly from economic development (GDP). It stands out, however, that the sourcing of resources has been shifted to other countries.

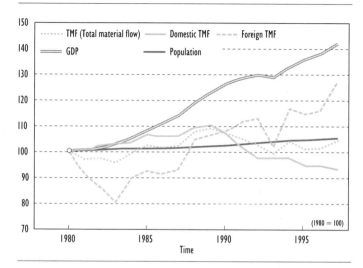

Figure 14 While the gross domestic product of the EU-15 has increased,
        the total consumption of natural resources TMF (total
        material flow) has remained roughly constant, however, at the
        expense of increased imports

Measured against the goal of dematerializing by a factor of
ten, the decoupling from economic development is still far from
sufficient. While the parasite's intelligence has improved in these
countries relative to GDP – the fundamental measure of economic accounting – unfortunately, the ecosphere, the host, is not
benefiting.

In developing countries, the absolute amount of resource extraction per capita is continuing to increase rapidly. But let us take
another look at the resource productivity of the countries in Europe.
Table 4 shows the current levels of national material productivity in
the EU-15 as well as the new member states of the EU and several
other countries for comparison. The productivity of a country is

given as the ratio of its gross domestic product to its direct material input (GDP/DMI). DMI is the sum of the resources extracted nationally plus the imports (without ecological rucksacks).

EU-15		Accession countries and non-EU countries	
Austria	1099	Norway	485
Belgium/Luxembourg	692	Bulgaria	76
Denmark	957	Cyprus	418
Finland	535	Czech Republic	163
France	1200	Estonia	57
Germany	1126	Hungary	329
Greece	578	Latvia	72
Ireland	724	Lithuania	109
Italy	1079	Malta	697
Netherlands	889	Poland	238
Portugal	583	Romania	128
Spain	709	Slovak Republic	199
Sweden	896	Slovenia	500
United Kingdom	1083	Turkey	328
EU-15 Total	1152	Average	226

Table 4 The countries of Europe display significant differences in the efficiency of their material use (resource productivity).

The accession countries and potential future member states must increase their productivity five-fold on average to attain the level of the EU-15

Apparently, there are differences of up to a factor of twenty (Germany/Estonia) between these countries. If Europe strives to serve as an example for ecological, and therefore also economic, sustainability, then these enormous differences should soon be a subject of negotiation.

The global economy's material flows

No economic area can be founded upon an autarchic resource base. Gigantic material flows cross all national borders in the form of raw materials, material goods, and food. As mentioned above, all these material objects carry larger or smaller ecological rucksacks with them, also crossing borders.

If we relate the Total Material Flow TMF to the population, then we have an indicator to compare regions and states with one another according to their ecological performance. Table 5 shows a comparison of the material metabolism in different countries and the European Union.

Portugal, Great Britain, and Japan have approximately half the resource consumption of the United States, Germany, and Finland. This alone should convince economic experts that resource consumption does not equal material prosperity.

The strong dependency of the Finnish economy on metals and materials is striking. It points to the particular strengths of the Finnish export industry: cell phones with different functions and heavy machinery for forestry. The high proportion of fossil energy carriers in Germany is also striking, and it contributes to the relatively high value for MI/kWh of the utilities' electricity mix.

The data presented here show that six different resource flows make up more than 90% of the total material input into the economy per capita in these countries and in the EU-15 (with the exception of The Netherlands), namely: fossil energy carriers (between 10 and 41% of TMF), metals, minerals, overburden, biomass (between 2 and 15% of TMF), and erosion (between 3 and 26% of TMF).

	D	J	USA	EU-15	NL	SF	UK	PL	China
Year	1999	1994	1994	1997	1993	1999	1999	1997	1996
DMI (metric tons per capita)	22	16	25	19	28	45	16	14	2
TMR (metric tons per capita)	71	45	85	51	67	98	41	32	37
% of TMF									
Non-renewable	90	94	93	88	90	79	85	90	98
Resources from other countries	38	56	7	39	72	47	92	23	1
Domestic resources not utilized	39	22	67	30	10	17	27	38	92
% of TMF									
Fossil energy carriers	41	28	37	29	22	10	33	40	22
Metals	20	20	11	20	4	27	21	10 } 22	17
Minerals	19	21	12	24	11	25	19		
Overburden	5	21	15	6	10	8	8	7	48
Biomass	10	6	7	12	10	21	15	10	2
Erosion	5	3	15	9	26	3	3	10	11
Other	1	1	2	1	17	5	1	0	1

Table 5 Material use, including ecological rucksacks, of different countries and the European Union

The population problem and resource consumption

Today's world population and its increase by approximately eighty million people per year are obstacles to be taken very seriously regarding achieving sustainable conditions at the global level.

More decisive than the sheer number of people is the per capita consumption of mass, energy, and land area in different strata of the world's population. The consumption of non-renewable natural resources by only approximately 20% of the world's population (the "rich") is higher than the ecologically sustainable level even today. While Germans consume an average of seventy metric tons of non-renewable resources per year, Vietnamese, for example, must make do with only three to four metric tons per year.

Every form of development of the economy today results in an increase of per capita consumption of natural resources. This increase is inflated additionally by the rising number of single people whose personal consumption of natural resources is two to four times higher than that of people living in "families."

Let us also remember the expected sea level rise caused by climate change. The possibly massive loss of built structures in coastal areas would imply an additional and very high demand for construction materials.

If we take the values for resource consumption calculated so far (national resource extraction plus imports plus their ecological rucksacks minus exports and their ecological rucksacks) for industrialized countries, and if we assume that these values were reached by all countries in the world over the course of the coming decades, with an expected global population of nine billion people, then, in the worst case, the Earth would have to yield up to five times the amount of resources (calculated without water and air), compared with current figures. As the ecological consequences of resource consumption are already too costly today, and the consumption of natural resources should be reduced by about half, this calculation, too, provides us with a pointer to the factor of ten.

For all these reasons, the radical improvement of the productivity of natural resources should be a top priority regarding solving demographic problems, too.

Boomerang effects

Dematerializing products and services is an essential precondition for the path to sustainability. But it is by no means the only precondition. The ecological advantage of a piece of clothing dematerialized by a factor of five, for example, is lost if five times as many pieces of clothing are brought to market. If the owners of ecologically excellent cars drive more kilometers per year than before, then they can fritter away the ecological advantage on account of higher mobility.

In other words, there is no direct connection between a successful increase in resource productivity at the level of processes, products and services on the one hand, and the total burden on the ecosphere on the other.

What counts from an ecological perspective is whether global resource consumption will be significantly lower in the future than it was at the beginning of the new millennium. The loss of efficiency gains achieved at the micro level of the economy by increased total consumption in an economic area is called the *boomerang* or *rebound* effect. Boomerang effects can be detected only by regularly measuring total resource flows through an economic area. And only measures on the macro level of the economy can reduce and prevent them. Governments must play a central role here.

Sustainable world trade?

In 1994, the World Trade Organization (WTO) was established as the successor to the GATT (General Agreement on Tariffs and Trade). More than one hundred countries around the world agreed on common rules for governing the international exchange of goods.

The WTO acts independently and has proven to be powerful because of its use of sanctions. It is concerned proactively with open market access and non-discrimination in transboundary trade. It seeks limitless trade, practically untouched by questions regarding the sustainability of the world's economy, and especially concerning the ecological consequences of trade between nations – although the preamble of its constitution has pointed out the significance of the use of natural resources in harmony with the goals of sustainable development and for the protection of the environment since the organization's founding in 1995.

The WTO does not act under the auspices or control of the United Nations. The foundation upon which the United Nations rests is the states' own commitments to the canon of human rights which are globally considered to be the highest universal legally protected interest. In the WTO treaties, in contrast, human rights are not mentioned. Article 103 of the Charter of the United Nations states explicitly: "In the event of a conflict between the obligations of the Members of the United Nations under the present Charter and their obligations under any other international agreement, their obligations under the present Charter shall prevail."

To the best of my knowledge, trade without boundaries is neither a basic human right nor a precondition for the sustainability of life on planet Earth. I would wish that trade, doubtless important in a market economy, would be subordinated to the basic demand of sustainability as quickly as possible, and in all of its dimensions: economic, social, and ecological.

"Unspoiled, undamaged, ruled by her own natural law and subject only to her own will – and the great void whence she sprang – the great Mother Earth took pleasure in creating and sustaining life in all its prolific diversity. But pillaged by a plundering dominion, raped of her resources, despoiled by unchecked pollution, and befouled by excess and corruption, her fecund ability to create and sustain could be undone. Though rendered sterile by destructive subjugation, her great productive fertility exhausted, the final irony would still be hers."

Jean M. Auel, *The Plains Of Passage*

The complexity of the economy and the ecosphere

One of Aesop's fables tells the story of the Greek shepherd boy who cried for help many a time without reason, with the consequence that nobody came to his aid when he actually did need help because a wolf was approaching. In the past thirty-five years, many well-meaning environmentalists have often and loudly cried wolf, thereby also contributing to the fact that normal people, but above all industry and governments, have become somewhat skeptical when confronted with forecasts about the types, extent, possible consequences, and costs of environmental problems.

The ecosphere is a highly complex web within which every-thing depends on many other things simultaneously, for which reason it is impossible to determine all the interrelationships. Science calls this type of web non-linear and complex. This means the following: when a small interference in this web trig-gers a small reaction, then that does not necessarily mean that a somewhat larger interference of the same kind triggers a some-what larger reaction. It may just as well be that the second reac-tion is principally different and more serious. The more complex the system, the less we can predict its reaction to stress.

It is impossible to grasp all the interrelationships in this web. Human interferences with the ecosphere cause an unknown number of reactions of unknown types and magnitudes and at often unknown locations.

I do not mean to imply that mankind should therefore lean back and observe the wonders of nature from a cautious dis-tance. We live in the midst of this ecosphere, change it constantly, and will continue to do so. But using technical means to provoke large-scale or even global changes, whether intentionally or not, is an experiment *in vivo*, as it were – tinkering with planet Earth and all its living creatures, including ourselves.

The realization that analysis cannot help us understand complex systems to such a degree that reliable forecasts about them can be made was something of a shock for the natural sci-ences in the 20th century. The physicist Heinz Pagels remarked in his book *The Dreams of Reason*: "Science has researched the micro- and the macrocosm. The big unknown is complexity."

The characteristics of parts of a complex web are insignificant if considered as isolated elements; they can be understood only in the context of the entire system, and the big picture is necessary for us to grasp their quantitative significance. The French philoso-pher René Descartes' conception that the whole can be explained by the sum of its parts, an idea considered valid for more than 400 years, has thus been proven wrong. Even if we understand the isolated parts ever so well, as soon as they are combined as a whole, something new emerges which can be understood only as a whole and which itself influences its parts. The characteristics of the parts disappear if the system is divided into little slices; theoretical or physical, political or institutional.

In light of the complexity of the ecosystem and the still precarious state of the data available at the global level concerning emissions and resource consumption caused by technologies, it should come as no surprise that the scientific community often has difficulty agreeing on statements about the type, location, extent, and danger of the ecological consequences of human activities. For example, twenty years ago, it was speculated that about the same amount of SO_2 escaped from technically crushed minerals as from the combustion of fossils containing sulfur – due to the effects on the crushed materials by oxygen in the air and rain. However, since not all paths of SO_2 in the environment can be traced in detail, many of its consequent impacts remain in the dark.

It is undisputed that the current structure of the global economy makes excessive demands of planet Earth. There is ample evidence to support this statement. For example, there is the partially disastrous collapse of deep-sea fishing; forested areas are on the decline and deserts are growing; since 2005, age-old walls on the slopes of Provence have been sliding downhill because they can no longer hold the weight of the waterlogged earth. Erosion of topsoil is increasing relentlessly. Groundwater tables in many areas are receding dangerously; ice caps and glaciers are turning into water; at the same time, the Aral Sea is drying out; and formerly great rivers are no longer carrying water.

For years, Camille Parmesan has been following how butterflies and other animals have been migrating northwards. While such geographic movements have not been unusual since time immemorial, current economic use of broad swathes of land have made it more difficult for animals and plants to move elsewhere. The evolutionary adaptation of animals and plants is also made impossible by mankind in its haste to subdue the Earth. Whether mankind, too, will take its leave from planet Earth's biosphere before its time remains to be seen.

Another reason why scientific prognoses of the ecological consequences of our actions are often difficult is that natural and man-made developments can overlap. This is the case when it comes to predicting and analyzing natural disasters, for example. Gases affecting the climate, such as CO_2 or methane, develop in large quantities by natural means. Climate research must therefore take them into account when calculating the consequences of emissions from the technosphere for the climate.

You yourself have surely noticed that scientists sometimes make contradictory statements or point out certain uncertainties in the debate about climate change. Serious media reporting about the effects of economic activity on the environment are therefore often introduced with qualifications such as: "scientists presume" or "the majority of experts agree." That is not evidence for the scientific community's shortcomings, but rather a proper indication of the natural limits of scientific knowledge.

The reader should therefore not be surprised that there are always people who disagree with their colleagues' opinions, even if the overwhelming majority has come to an agreement about certain findings. On the one hand, such arguments are important in order not to suppress remaining disagreements. In addition, this may well be a legitimate way for usually younger colleagues to attract attention. Some individuals even build their careers on such contradictions.

But it seems particularly important to me that, for the reasons mentioned, politicians have no choice but to make decisions even in light of incomplete scientific knowledge. Little in the business of politics irritates me more than the routine refusal of decision-makers to act by pointing out that the scientific community has not yet finally settled the matter – especially when existing alternative options to act are undisputedly of a preventive nature, have been decided in democratic processes, and can be integrated into existing structures at reasonable cost.

Incidentally, even today, forecasts about climate change are more precise than the prognoses of the six leading German institutes for economics regarding the country's economic development in the coming years. Maybe it is time to establish a number of well-funded institutes for sustainability to become better informed about the ecological changes and their possible consequences for economic development in Europe.

The devastations caused by hurricanes

To this day, nobody has seriously alleged that all the hurricanes of the year 2005 were due to our resource-intensive lifestyle. But likewise, nobody could seriously doubt that their number and intensity were linked to developments triggered by mankind. One way or the other, 'natural disasters' have increased fourfold in the last forty years.

As a reminder, and to better understand the economic and social consequences of 'natural disasters,' let us bring to mind the wide-ranging consequences of the monster hurricane Katrina that descended upon Mississippi and Louisiana in the southern United States in late August of 2005.

After several days of advance warning, Katrina devastated

large portions of the states of Louisiana and Mississippi. Damage was sustained in an area the size of Great Britain. Indirect effects reached regions far inland. The first days were marked by total confusion and helplessness. And this occurred, even though the US had established an extensive and expensive disaster response system after the collapse, caused by terrorists, of the twin towers of the World Trade Center in New York on September 11 four years before. Katrina was one reason why popular support of the President's work diminished markedly. And it also reopened the rifts between black and white because the poor in the affected areas did not have sufficient possibilities of reaching shelter.

One week after Katrina, official sources estimated the death toll at several thousand. For weeks, access to previously inhabited areas was possible only by boat, especially in metropolitan New Orleans, home to more than one million people; electricity and water supply for those who had remained – mostly blacks – was interrupted. The government made more than 50 billion US dollars available in the first ten days as an initial tranche (this corresponds to approximately 17% of the German federal budget). Reconstruction costs have been estimated to total at least 200 billion US dollars. How long reconstruction would take could not be assessed even months after the disaster.

Katrina had far-reaching effects on the commodity market. For example, coffee prices rose by 10% because warehouses in New Orleans Harbor were destroyed. The price of wood increased by 17% during the first weeks after Katrina. Significant effects on the price of grain were expected as well because more than half of US grain exports go through New Orleans Harbor. The potential economic effects weakened the value of the dollar and drove up the price of metals, especially the price of gold, which has been rising constantly since then. Copper hit a high of 3725 dollars per metric ton on September 2, 2005. Cargo rates for fuel tankers from Europe to the US increased by 60 percent in the week following Katrina.

The most severe effects of Katrina, however, were on the energy sector. The prices for oil, oil products, and natural gas reached record levels and have not settled down since then. The price of oil rose to more than 70 US dollars per barrel. According to Deutsche Bank, fuel costs have now risen to approximately 5% of disposable income in the US, placing significantly higher burdens on low-income households. The distinct changes in private purchasing decisions and use of automobiles since then have contributed to considerable instabilities for the large American car manufacturers on the domestic market. On June 28, 2006, the *Herald Tribune* ran the following headline on page one: "For the US, Smart's time has come." The article reported on DaimlerChrysler's plan to put the compact car on the US market in 2008.

In contrast to the consumers, oil companies have reaped unprecedented profits since Katrina, even though their drilling and refining facilities were severely damaged by the hurricane. Possibly the most important effect on the energy market, however, could be that natural gas futures increased by 20% in the first week after the storm. In contrast to crude oil and fuels, there are no emergency stocks which could be shared with other countries.

Just two weeks after Katrina, hurricane Rita devastated the same area anew. New Orleans was flooded again, even if less so than by Katrina. Millions of people were driven inland again.

In the past thirty-five years, some life-threatening dangers to human life caused by technology have been recognized at a fairly early stage. Climate change is surely the most well-known example. The history of its discovery reaches back to the mid-19th century. But experts' broad agreement on its possible extent and effects is hardly more than ten years old. Since Mojib Latif describes the entire history of climate change in *Climate Change: The Point of No Return* in this series, I will not pursue the topic further here.

Another potential threat recognized early on was the decomposition of the Earth's ozone layer, which protects the planet from dangerous solar radiation, by synthetically created chlorofluorocarbons (CFCs). For decades, people had trusted in the chemical inertness of these gases and therefore ruled out the possibility of danger to the environment. Then, in the early 1970s, while Sherry Rowland was carrying out experiments for entirely different reasons in his laboratory, he happened across the phenomenon and later received a Nobel Prize for his brilliant interpretation of it. In the meantime, the use of CFCs has been limited worldwide, and observations seem to indicate that the hole in the ozone layer is shrinking.

My impression is that the international agreement on effective countermeasures – even if delayed by years – is founded above all on the fact that human health is affected directly, for example because of higher rates of skin cancer in Australia. In addition, the losses of production due to the ban on CFCs could be compensated by other chemicals less hazardous to the environment.

Another development with serious consequences for Europe seems to be looming: the Gulf Stream might weaken, it could even shut down completely in its current form in the north. Since time immemorial, it has been transporting warm water from the Gulf of Mexico to the Arctic Sea, where it sinks down after giving off its warmth and flows back south as a cold deep water mass. This sinking, induced by changes in temperature, is the actual motor of the Gulf Stream. There are firm indications that the Gulf Stream, a "conveyor belt of warmth," came to a standstill several times in the distant past. The newest measurements show that is has lost approximately 30% of its power in the past ten years.

The 'conveyor belt of warmth' provides the northwestern parts of Europe with a relatively mild climate. Amsterdam, for example, is at the same latitude as the northernmost tip of the island of Newfoundland in Canada, but in comparison, the city's climate is mild. If the new measurements indicate a permanent condition, northwestern Europe will likely have to reckon with an average cooling of 1 °C. If the Gulf Stream continues to lose power, the consequences could be more unpleasant and much more expensive.

The basis of the hypothesis of the Gulf Stream's heating capacity possibly petering out is, curiously enough, global warming. Due to rising temperatures, the ice masses in Greenland are melting, and rivers in the far north are carrying more water. In this way, enormous amounts of water with a low salt content enter the Gulf Stream where it sinks down to lower levels. The fresh water has a significantly lower density than the cold brine of the Gulf Stream arriving there. As the two mix, the power of the "sinking motor" is diminished, and as a consequence, the cycle of the Gulf Stream could be weakened.

Skeptics will rightly point out that measurements have been indicating a weakening of the Gulf Stream for only a few years. But the results of the measurements are as firm as possible with today's science. They show definite deviations from the previously stable situation and should induce countries such as Portugal, Spain, France, the Benelux countries, Ireland, Great Britain, Germany, and western Scandinavia to follow the development closely and to put considerable effort into seeking sustainable solutions for their populations and economies.

Providing the world with food is also a cause for legitimate concern. Not only is the world's population growing by approximately 80 million people per year, with an additional need for about 0.5 hectares per person (Germany has about 0.45 hectares available per person, but uses significant land area in other countries for food imported from there). At present, we invest about five times more energy in food production than we get in return in the form of energy contained in crops. In a manner of speaking, we are subsidizing the harvest of solar energy captured today by plants with fossil energy, in other words, with "frozen" energy that was captured by other plants hundreds of millions of years ago. This is certainly not a sustainable way of feeding the world's population.

Scientists at the International Rice Research Institute in the Philippines and their colleagues at the United States Department of Agriculture predict that every degree of temperature increase during the growing season could diminish the global harvests of wheat, rice, and corn by approximately 10%. A number of other changes in the environment also have negative effects on the production of food. They include the expansion of deserts, the land area needed for mobility – which is on the rise globally – erosion, and the increasing scarcity of water. Expanding deserts can be found, for example, in Brazil (approximately 60 million hectares of desert today), China (increase of approximately 360,000 hectares per year), India (approximately 100 million hectares today, or around one-third of the country's land area), and Nigeria (increase of approximately 350,000 hectares per year). In the east and north of China, 24,000 villages have either been given up entirely or have lost significant proportions of their populations because of the encroaching desert.

According to the United Nations Environment Programme (UNEP), advancing desertification is affecting the living conditions of one billion people in more than 100 countries around the world. The situation is especially critical in North America and Africa. There, 70% of the arid areas under agricultural cultivation are damaged or threatened by desertification. The consequences are a rural exodus, hunger, and poverty. UNEP estimates the costs due to the expansion of deserts worldwide at 42 billion US dollars per year.

Poverty is not only a consequence of desertification, but also one of its most important causes. Too much is extracted from the soil, trees are cut down for firewood, there is too much fertilization and too many cattle, and droughts contribute to the dire situation as well. Experts estimate that every year, 25 billion metric tons of fertile soil are lost due to erosion.

Since 1950, the global fleet of automobiles has increased by a factor of ten to more than 500 million cars, of which 80% are driven in industrialized countries. In the United States, using a car needs a total of 0.07 hectares; at two million additional vehicles per year, this adds up to a requirement of 140,000 more hectares of land annually. Even today, 16 million hectares of land are devoted to automobile use in the United States. For comparison, in 2004, wheat was grown on 21 million hectares.

In China, India, Indonesia, Bangladesh, Pakistan, Iran, Egypt, and Mexico, which together are home to approximately 50% of the world's population, it will not be possible to attain the same vehicle density as in Europe, Japan, or North America without losing critical amounts of arable land.

Approximately 5% of the world's agricultural land is

under acute threat from erosion by wind and water. Controlling erosion is possible in many cases, but requires substantial financial means which are not available in most of the affected countries. The worldwide loss of arable land is estimated at approximately 130,000 hectares per year, or about half the area of the Saarland. In addition, the expected sea level rise may limit the availability of land for food production (in Bangladesh, for example, this is a decisive factor). At the same time, the effects of floods during the rainy season on land used for economic purposes are becoming noticeably more frequent in many regions of the world. There are a number of reasons for this. Even a temperature shift of less than 1 °C in mountainous regions results in less snowfall and more rain instead. This also means less long-term storage and slow release of water by snow and glaciers. This effect is augmented by the soils' diminished capacity to hold precipitation because heavy machinery used for agriculture and forestry has compacted the earth, and because of large-scale clear-cutting.

Human beings require approximately four liters of drinking water per day to live. However, 500 times that amount of water is used to produce the food that each one of us needs per day. On average, 1000 metric tons of water are needed to produce one metric ton of grain, and in the large cotton growing areas of the former Soviet Union and the United States, it takes more than thirty metric tons of water to produce 0.001 metric tons (one kilogram) of cotton.

Globally, the difference between the additional demand for water and its sustainable supply is growing bigger by the day. Hardly anywhere is agriculture in a financial position to assert its claims for more water vis-à-vis growing demands on the part of urban areas and industry. The solution to this problem cannot lie in even greater subsidies for agriculture. Especially in this sector

of the economy, *full-cost pricing* will be of significant importance for approaching sustainable framework conditions.

Year	Total (km³)	Population (millions)	Agriculture (%)	Industry (%)	Urban use (%)
1700	110	700	90	2	8
1800	243	1000	90	3	7
1900	580	1600	90	6	3
1950	1360	2500	83	13	4
1970	2590	3500	72	22	5
1990	4130	5300	66	24	8
2000*	5190	6000	64	25	9

Table 6 Global withdrawal of water in cubic kilometers, increase in
the world's population, and percentages used by agriculture,
industry, and cities since 1700

*Extrapolated

Table 6 shows the tempestuous development of the withdrawal of fresh water at the global level since 1700 for the most
important areas of use. In the last decade of the last century,
Asia was responsible for 60%, North America for 18%, Europe
for 13%, Africa for 6%, and South America for 4 percent. Evidently, people use an average of 5.5 times as much water today
as their forbears did around 1700.

As surface water is no longer available for food production in
many regions, and some large rivers in Asia barely carry water
any more, more and more groundwater is being pumped up. In
countries with more than half the world's population, the withdrawal of water from wells exceeds natural renewal of the aqui-
fers. In the United States, the depletion of the Ogallala aquifer,
which spreads across large parts of the Midwest, is a cause for
concern. In northern China, the groundwater tables are falling

by three to four meters per year. This has been a decisive contributing factor for China becoming a net importer of rice in the last few years. In most states of India, groundwater tables are falling, especially in the important agricultural areas of Punjab and Haryana. For this reason, India is experiencing growing difficulties in feeding 18 million additional people per year. Israel and Palestine, Yemen and Iran, Saudi Arabia as well as Mexico also belong to the countries with groundwater problems.

A growing number of scientists considers the economic effects of the increasing scarcity of water to be significantly more severe than the dwindling oil reserves. Lester Brown of the Worldwatch Institute says, "There are substitutes for oil, but not for water. Mankind lived for 6 million years without oil. Without water, we would be finished after a few days."

This brief characterization of the growing problems of food supply makes clear that not only the productivity of materials, but also that of water and land must be improved decisively.

The Kyoto Protocol – the path to the future?

Have you ever had this experience? Dead tired, after three or four nights spent working. Surrounded by the hustle and bustle of thousands of more or less official lobbyists from around the globe who represent a thousand different interests and are pursuing a thousand different goals; constantly sought after by hundreds of journalists – after all, you are a representative of a powerful country – worn down long ago and ready for a compromise that contributes to move the great affair forward at least a little bit; always anxious not to aggravate the Americans, for God's sake; dependent on English-speaking colleagues for assistance with wording in order to build a nascent coalition with dozens of mother tongues, because all that counts in the end is what is on paper in English? And then, suddenly, after all the frustration, after countless cups of coffee and never-ending hand-to-hand combat rations, suddenly the exhilaration of having succeeded and formulated an acceptable Protocol after all. A moment of pride, for having in some way played a part, for having struggled for a just cause under the most difficult circumstances, and for having had a hand in one or two wordings that include the reasonably represented main concerns of one's own faction. You are happy, you celebrate, because you joined with new friends from faraway lands in struggling for words, and together you are still angry with certain representatives of "stubborn" countries who made everything so difficult. A moment of triumph at the end of the travails, and mutual congratulations are appropriate. Now the minister can face the cameras in a remote land and proclaim success on television. And yet – even during the initial celebrations, you get the sneaking feeling that maybe it isn't as earth-shattering as it seems.

Almost ten years after the Kyoto Protocol was signed, more than 10,000 people from 200 countries and territories had flocked to Montreal in 2005 to argue about a few more percent of emission reductions for a handful of substances that had been identified as the main causes of climate change. And what came of all this? The promise to desire to continue negotiating with the goal of achieving additional reductions of climate-effective emissions, above and beyond the 5% reduction agreed on back in 1997. Even the representatives of the United States generously consented to participate in these talks.

It is not yet certain whether the 5% reductions, originally agreed on for fifteen years, can be achieved by 2012. After all, the US declared even in 2001 that they would not contribute towards this common achievement. And the Chinese, too, are staying at the margins. Yet these two countries are responsible for more than 40% of the total technology-induced emissions of CO_2. US President George Bush said in 2001 that reducing emissions according to the Kyoto Protocol would ruin his country's economy. This may have been the unintended insight that "end-of-pipe" measures *after* acknowledging certain environmental dangers are very expensive.

In the Kyoto Protocol, ratified by Germany in 2002, many of the important industrialized countries committed in concrete terms to reduce their emissions significantly in the years 2008 to 2012, compared with the base year 1990. Even before the first conference in Kyoto in 1997, the overwhelming majority of thousands of scientists from around the globe had warned that only a reduction of at least 60% of global climate-relevant emissions would provide the opportunity to stabilize climate change at a possibly bearable level. A recent study by the Pentagon agrees with this as well. This goal cannot be attained without comprehensive structural change of the economy. But that is not a subject that the environment ministers are authorized to negotiate about.

More than ten years have now passed since the preparations for the Kyoto conference began in 1997. The conference was to bring about a decisive reduction of climate-relevant emissions, and in a foreseeable period of time. If we take what has actually been achieved since then as a yardstick, then a hundred years will pass until the ecologically-necessary emission reductions will have been agreed upon and complied with in a verifiable way. There may well be grounds to assume that a considerable part of the problem of emitting climate-relevant substances will, in a manner of speaking, have taken care of itself because of the increasing scarcity of fossil fuels. Some experts consider the social and economic consequences of the currently foreseeable trend to be extremely negative.

After all that we have discussed so far, the reader may well rub his or her eyes and ask in bewilderment: why don't we use innovative technology on the input side of the economy in order to reduce emissions on the output side? – particularly since we know that it is technically feasible, that it makes sense economically, and that we could also get a handle on considerable elements of the problems of unemployment and national debt at the same time?

The 30-year-old Brundtlandt Report was a historic breakthrough for gaining a future with a future for humankind. What we have learned since then is that the economy is doomed unless it functions within the guardrails of the ecosphere. An economy which does not take the laws of nature seriously, destroys itself.

Sustainable solutions?

As the Brundtland Commission of the United Nations had proclaimed even ten years before the first conference on climate change in Kyoto – and ceremoniously confirmed in 1992 in Rio de Janeiro by all countries – successful steps towards sustainability are possible only if societal, economic, and ecological concerns are taken into account at the same time and granted the same importance. To this day, however, none of the organizational units of the United Nations are responsible for this issue. Within the frameworks of their assigned competences, they are all fighting for their particular interests independently of one another. The Sixth WTO Ministerial Conference, held in Hong Kong in December 2005, was devoted exclusively to the topic of making world trade run as smoothly as possible – entirely independent of the consumption of natural resources.

Neither in the European Commission in Brussels nor in

Germany, France, or other European countries, large or small, is there an institution that is politically responsible for sustainability and that has the means to enforce what is necessary.

The American news station CNN reminds us hour by hour that the United States and a number of allied countries are intensely engaged in a war on terrorism. The natural resources devoted to the war in Iraq alone would have been sufficient to build housing for a billion people. But the US is constantly demanding exactly the kind of solidarity from all countries for this war that it is vehemently denying for the protection of the common ecosphere. Perhaps the US should realize that many people today regard the country's excessive resource consumption as an attack on the physical and emotional well-being of billions of people in other countries. But not only the US must give serious thought to the worldwide consequences of the west's consumption of nature.

The current global circus of huge international conferences seems to rest on the hope that we can solve isolated problems with traditional means – following traditional competences of ministries – and that we have plenty of time to do so. Once we have worked out solutions for global social, ecological, fiscal and economic problems in a parallel fashion – this seems to be the hope – then we could harmonize them with one another. But this hope is unfounded. For one thing, it does not correspond to historic experience, and it overlooks the fact that it is systemically impossible to remedy the fundamental mistakes of the economy by means of individual reactive measures.

6 Services And Their Utility

When people talk about services provided by people, we immediately understand what they mean. Everyone can name a large number of jobs in the service sector, and everyone uses the services of the German railways. Services are increasingly also provided directly by machines which threaten jobs, for example automatic teller machines. Aside from a few basic needs, such as a bed, clothing, a roof over one's head as well as sufficient food, people actually need only services.

The concept of services, however, is not limited to man and technology. Nature, too, is a provider of services, for example, the sun shines, bees pollinate blossoms, the air cleanses itself, and nutrients regenerate in the soil. As we have already seen, life as we know it is not possible without such services. Their special advantage lies in the fact that we pay nothing at all for them. Their particular disadvantage is that they are affected by our economic system.

In the following, we will consider services and the utilities they each provide. And finally, we will examine how and where we can find ecologically sensible utility and how the technology of tomorrow can provide that utility.

Practical services

In general, we consider services to be the work of cleaning crews or workshops, public transportation, financial or management consulting firms, nurses, or hairdressers – in other words, work carried out by people for other people. Following this concept, services are all those kinds of work whose goal is not the production of a material object we can grasp with our hands, but rather help, consultation, or organization.

That is at least the traditional way of talking about services. The classical definition says that services of the technosphere are immaterial goods. But it is obvious that these immaterial goods can only actually exist, that we are only able to take advantage of them, if equipment and machines are available to produce the services. After all, a trip is possible only if we can make use of a bicycle, an airplane, or a dogsled. And a grandmother can read her grandson a bedtime story only if a lamp, a bed, a warm room, and a book are available.

For all intents and purposes, industrial products are needed only if they are actually used. Using means gaining utility from products or their service capacity. Accordingly, people don't actually purchase products, but rather service machines. This applies to a shower just as to a microwave, a sofa, an automobile, a telephone, or a freezer.

In other words, services depend on existing service machines and often consume energy during their use. Without energy supply, without infrastructures, buildings, and a multitude of different machines and equipment, there would be no service sector. Modern societies are characterized by a large number of services and by their high quality; the services are dependent upon a network that functions like clockwork.

Using goods and facilities means availing oneself of the

services they provide. It follows from this that the quality of life people can attain depends on the variety and quality of services they can take advantage of. In a social market economy, people who are sick or needy also have access to food and services.

In order to enjoy services, one does not necessarily have to own the appropriate products. I pointed this out earlier in this book. For example, only few people buy an airplane for their next vacation. But it is not uncommon for people to get an electric drill as a Christmas present even though they too, use it only rarely. If we assume that one out of every fifteen Germans owns such a tool, then more than 10,000 metric tons of high-quality material are frozen within them, and far more than twenty times that amount of environment would be consumed even before they reach the retailer.

We can also borrow or rent service machines, or pay others to use their machines for our needs. However, the fact that we do not need to own things to enjoy their services does not mean that we do not derive contentment, happiness, and joy from the things we do own. I, for one, consider it very important, to own my own bed and dining table. Things are different, however, when it comes to high-pressure cleaners, skiing equipment, and automobiles.

If we consider in detail the multitude of industrial products we possess, we will discover, to our wonderment, that we allow ourselves material luxury that is entirely absurd from a financial perspective and other points of view. A Finnish lady, living alone, found out that she owned far more than 7000 different objects. After she had divided them into groups according to whether she used or enjoyed them at least once a week, once a year, or practically never, she got rid of more than half of her belongings and is now enjoying much more space in her small apartment.

To confuse the concept of service even more, businesses also call the services they offer "products." For instance, your bank's offer to take care of all your investments comprehensively, or an "all-included" vacation package are considered such "products." Today, you can also purchase the products "heat," "cold," or "lighting," both for your business and your private needs. And no industrial product is on offer today that does not also require service as an input for its manufacturing and use. For industrial products with a long life span, the proportion of service inputs shifts from the production phase to the usage phase.

Luxury and resources

Jewelry, perfume, fashionable clothing, paintings, and musical instruments also serve the purpose of conveying contentment, happiness, and joy. So they, too, are among the products whose use brings service or utility. Whether or not they number among deepest desires, or whether a high quality of life can be reached through their availability, is not our concern in this book.

From an ecological point of view, for example, a painting is interesting because it requires only a small amount of natural resources "from the cradle to the grave." The rucksack of a medium-sized painting by Miotte or Matisse, including the frame (without gold and silver!), weighs only approximately forty kilograms, and it hardly requires any additional resources to convey pleasure to its viewers for hundreds of years. Its MIPS is minute, in other words.

If we assume the price of such a painting to be 400,000 euros, then the ratio of its price to its ecological rucksack is approximately 20,000 times greater than that of a mid-sized car. Apparently, creative artists have a high appreciation for natural resources.

Now, there are also things whose *raison d'être* lies to a considerable degree in making an impression on other people. They include, for instance: Rolls-Royce cars, fur coats, racehorses, twenty-meter yachts at Saint Tropez, luxury villas, or decorations such as the Order of Merit of the Federal Republic of Germany. But I gladly leave it up to the reader to decide whether these things, too, also provide utility.

Services performed by machines

At the very least, when we get annoyed by public transportation ticket machines, we begin to realize that services for people are increasingly provided directly by machines. And cash is now also available from a machine at midnight. All over the world, such services provided by machines are more and more on the increase. Surfing in internet cafés in Ubud on Bali is almost as important today as the skillful massage of aching feet.

To summarize: (1) Service is the characteristic of goods, based on appreciation, to provide utility or satisfaction of a need. (2) Products that do not require service as an input do not exist, and there are no services without products. (3) In the economy, services are provided by people for people, or by machines for people. (4) Nature pays a price for every service. (5) The ecological rucksack of services is the sum of the prorated ecological rucksacks of the equipment, vehicles, and buildings used, plus the sum of the prorated consumption of materials and energy during the use of this equipment and of these vehicles and buildings.

From the concept of the term "service" presented here, it was only a small step to using it in the definition of a metric for the ecological relevance of products and actions of any kind as we do in the term MIPS (see Chapter 3).

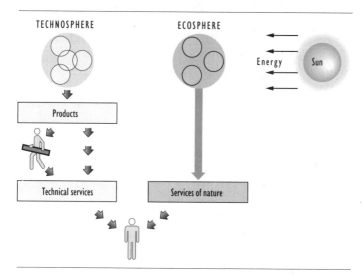

Figure 15 Within the technosphere, services are provided to customers
either directly by machines, or by people making use of
products, infrastructures, and energy when providing services

Without exception, services within the technosphere can be provided *only* by
consuming nature. On the other hand, the *ecosphere* provides services to
humans cost-free. Without these services of nature, humankind cannot survive
on earth.

Nature's services

Up to this point in this chapter, I have dealt only with services
that are part of the economy and are provided using technology.
I have described how they open the path to utility and prosperity.
Perhaps I even conveyed the impression that all prosperity is a
question of human development. However, that is not the case.

In previous chapters, I spoke repeatedly about the services provided by nature (see Glossary) and their paramount significance

for the survival and well-being of human beings on planet Earth. What differentiates these two types of services from one another?

Without the services of nature, as they have developed over the course of billions of years, we humans would never have evolved. Our survival depends on their functioning. We may be able to change the services of the ecosphere by means of our economic processes, but we can neither increase nor "improve" them by technology. The services of the ecosphere are indivisible. Neither can a person use nature's services for just herself or himself, nor can people damage them without other people having to bear the consequences as well.

In a nutshell, people's access to technology-based services costs money, is functionally adapted to individual needs, and can be improved by means of economic, social, and technical developments, but cannot be devised without natural resources. Not all technology-based services are vital. The services of the ecosphere, on the other hand, are all, without exception, necessary for sustaining human life. They are available for free, cannot be increased by means of technology, and are damaged locally and globally as a consequence of unwise economic management. Apart from that, services of the ecosphere are by definition not provided by machines or human beings.

The utility of life

The highest utility of human life is to achieve contentment, happiness and joy, in safety and dignity, and to share accomplishments with others. However, pursuing these aims also involves costs. This book is mainly concerned with the costs borne by the ecosphere. As we have already seen, these costs must be kept as low as at all possible in order to secure our future.

Achieving and maintaining a high quality of life for themselves and their families in security – in the physical, emotional, spiritual, and also material sense – may be the most natural desire people can have. Increasing utility, therefore, is a kind of growth, defined via people's quality of life.

Achieving contentment, happiness, and joy requires access to sufficient food and also to the use of material goods and institutions such as hospitals and retirement homes. This holds for people with very modest needs as well. Nobody wants to live without clothing to provide warmth, without hygiene, a roof, a bed, or without a dentist's practice. Accordingly, one can define utility as a metric for the ability of goods to satisfy people's needs.

I called the ecological price of utility MIPS. One can also consider MIPS the ecological metric for the provision of services. As we have already seen, this is not possible in a modern society without using products, not even if the services are provided by people. Therefore, we can also speak of technology-based service here. That also holds for the use of natural products, because only in a few rare instances do natural products arrive at our doorstep without technical processing, packaging, storage, and transportation.

The traditional doctrine that everlasting growth is necessary on economic grounds causes two problems now. Firstly, the costs of the ecosphere for human utility cannot increase endlessly because our planet Earth has physical limits. And secondly, I lack the imagination to visualize what the amplification of contentment, happiness, and joy might be.

The more people in a society who attain the desired utility in the sense described above, the higher we can consider a society's prosperity to be. Understood in this way, prosperity means much more than material wealth. It also includes things such as education, health, security, work, leisure time, and environmental quality.

While in our present-day production society, the focus is on products, the service provided by a product will be at the center of attention in a service-based society. In other words, viewed from an economic point of view, it will not be the material value, the physical nature of an object that determines the economic value, but the object's use value or service value. For this reason, it may very well be profitable for businesses not to sell primarily the material product, but rather its use, and to achieve a financial profit with the help of the factor time. No longer will the stylish sports car be sold, but the service of driving it and maybe making an impression.

In this vein, the Ender company in Vorarlberg, Austria successfully sells the use of air-conditioning technology to customers large and small (office@ender-klimatechnik.com). Of course, this requires that we consumers develop a relationship to material goods that is based more on the result than on ownership. This in turn necessitates that entrepreneurs must take on the risk of an unaccustomed system conversion. And this, finally, presupposes that loans for small and medium-sized enterprises must be adapted to the fact that cash flow patterns are different from previous ones.

On the demand side, the political and business communities have decidedly promoted preferences for ownership of material goods at least since the middle of the last century. One need only look at advertising – by Bosch, Siemens, and Toyota, or home loan banks – or the write-offs permitted by tax law to recognize this fact. One's own electric drill, washing machine, car, house, for some even one's own yacht are unconditionally desirable, as if by reflex, even if in many cases, their ownership actually lies with the bank.

I have observed that people prefer ownership of service machines because they can then enjoy using them at any time they wish, and because scheduling things often becomes simpler and more convenient. Above and beyond that, a far-reaching lack of awareness of the costs per service unit makes a practical comparison of the costs for using one's own equipment with the costs of services difficult. That seems to be one reason why consumers and even businesses do not take full advantage of the services offered by service providers.

Focusing on utility helps to create a future with a future

As we have seen when discussing MIPS, focusing on the utility of products and services can help to take new directions in creating sustainable prosperity. For example, such a focus can be useful for changing economic concepts of value as well as priorities, to give a new meaning to growth – namely increasing utility – to explore paths to sustainability that focus on utility instead of on owning objects. New models for work and progress, for urban planning, development aid, and for living together in society could be developed, and new products and services that use small amount of resources could be designed. Patterns of consumption can be guided towards sustainability in this way, easing the transition to a "service society." And last, but certainly not least, a strategy can be developed and put into practice in Europe, and spread throughout the world that can contribute to securing the future of mankind on planet Earth.

The Factor 10/MIPS concept does not require limiting consumption highhandedly or even prohibiting it because consumption is material-intensive. Rather, it is a positive approach: It requires seeking possibilities to provide appropriate services where services are needed, but with considerably lower material consumption.

As we have already seen, we can influence the ecological costs of services from two angles, namely from both the demand and the supply side. For instance, vacation-seekers can prefer staying on a farm in Franconia to a flight to Florida. Or we can use the towel in a hotel bathroom for three days in a row. On the supply side, the travel company or hotel can select objects, equipment, and facilities that are as resource-efficient as possible, both for their business operations and for their customers during their vacations. And hospital operators could offer outpatient services rather than inpatient ones.

Let us put this rule to the test. The next time we want to purchase something, let us scrutinize our intentions: exactly which service do we want to have, and how much of it is necessary, when is the service to be provided, and for how long?

To try this out, let us compare our current service-providing machine for mobility – our car – with the actual transportation or mobility needs of the family. How large is the difference between the vehicle's maximum performance and what we need, and what traffic permits in the first place? When was the last time we drove to work, to buy cigarettes, or to the dentist at 180 kilometers per hour? Maximum speed in city traffic is between ten and fifty kilometers per hour, and the actual average is considerably less than twenty, sometimes even less than ten kilometers per hour. How often are five people in the car? How many hours per day does the car do what it was built to do, namely to transport people and things? Insurance, liability insurance, and costs for the garage accrue twenty-four hours a day. And if we park on the street, then we subsidize ourselves via the tax system: after all, roads cost a lot of money. So what does each kilometer we drive actually cost? Sixty euro cents? Eighty euro cents? In any case, we consume 300 grams of environment or more for every kilometer, not including the highly resource-intensive infrastructure in our calculation.

Might it pay off to consider the zero ownership option, that is, to rent or lease a car or to use a taxi when we need one? Then, we can even choose between a vehicle for city driving (Citycar) that seats two and a larger sedan for weekends and vacations with the family. If we drive only half as much as today, a taxi with a driver would probably be cheaper – provided the car is not purchased on credit. In that case, the taxi would definitely be cheaper.

But is the bundle of services that fulfills our mobility needs even on offer today? Probably not, at least not at an appropriate price. Now the question arises: why not? The market economy should be able to satisfy such a demand by offering new services, shouldn't it?

Choosing the best

In early sections of this book, we learned that increasing ecological utility can occur only with the help of products that are produced, transported, traded, stored, and used with high resource productivity. Therefore, the goal of ecological consumption is to seek the ecologically and economically most effective ways to fulfill a particular function or satisfy a particular need. As regards food, resource efficiency and intensity of erosion play a major role in addition to their contamination with toxic substances.

Deliberate moderate behavior is always distinguished by high resource productivity and financial savings. In the case of tending your lawn, preserving the biological diversity of flowers, butterflies, and insects is of interest as well. In my opinion, bans and requirements are not desirable measures for saving resources. Not only does it cost a lot of money to administer them, they also result in limitations on the freedom to make decisions, and they weaken self-reliance. As you have already seen in this book, I always support guiding resource savings by means of ecologically realistic prices. Having developed legal instruments myself, I am not a great believer in detailed government regulations or a planned economy.

Making difficult choices

How can the average consumer know how ecologically costly or ecologically inexpensive a service-providing machine really is? Information according to the MIPS concept is normally not available as yet, and existing labeling is, as we have seen, not really all that helpful. In any case, it will be difficult, if not practically impossible, to make ecologically sensible decisions about purchasing or using goods and services. In the following, we would nonetheless like to assemble a list of questions that can help us to track down the ecologically better alternative. We encountered a few of them some time ago, and have long been taking others into account, consciously or not.

As has already been emphasized: first, we have to know the characteristics of the "bundle of services" we desire; and second, we need to have justified to ourselves what we really need, when, for how long, and how much of it.

In the following list, the term "good" can mean anything that we can grasp and that can provide utility, from a mousetrap to flowers to a house.

How much material does the good consume when it is being used? This may refer to fuel, detergent, lubricants, cleaning agents, water, and the like. How much electricity does it consume during use? What is the guaranteed and what is the actually expected life-time? How big is the good? How much does it weigh? How much surface area does it require? Are smaller models with sufficient performance characteristics available? What distance did the good travel, and by which means of transportation, before it was offered to me? Is the packaging appropriate, can it be re-used? What metals are contained in it and how much of each? Can parts be recycled?

These are the most important questions, and perhaps also the ones that are the most difficult to answer. Usually, neither the retailer nor the consumer knows the material composition of the good, nor can they estimate the ecological rucksacks, in other words, they cannot know how much environment went into producing all the different materials that the good is composed of. How much recyclable or renewable material does the good contain? As functionally comparable units are frequently similar, the weight of two cars or two sewing machines can serve as an initial rough indication. But we should not rely on it.

- Does the good reliably monitor and optimize itself, for example by means of electronic control of the influx of consumables (energy, water, detergent, etc.)?
- Can the good be used to satisfy different needs? Is it multifunctional?
- Can the good still serve other purposes or other people when I can no longer use it for its original purpose?

– Can I lend or rent the good to others to use; is it robust enough to do so?
– How durable is the good? What is the length of the guarantee period?

Knowing about the following characteristics also helps us assess the durability of goods:

Surface characteristics (wear, cleaning), corrosion resistance, repairability, shape, and ease of disassembly (for maintenance and repairs), robustness, reliability. Products should be designed in such a way that individual components can be exchanged for new state-of-the-art ones (for instance, drive assemblies in vehicles or printed circuit boards in computers).

Of course, this list is much too long to be fun, and your retailer will certainly only have some of the answers. MIPS-type labeling would make things much simpler. But if enough people persist in asking such questions, then maybe it will help move sustainability a small step forward. We consumers are kings in the market economy, aren't we?

We should consider very seriously whether the following information should be provided on all finished products in the future: country of manufacture, ecological rucksack, MIPS, and known harmful substances that the product contains or that can be formed during the product's use.

The new Kondratiev wave

Sigmar Gabriel, the German Federal Minister for the Environment, made the following statement in an article in the German daily newspaper *Süddeutsche Zeitung* of January 9, 2006 titled "Energy and Raw Material Intelligence – Questions that will decide our future": "There is every indication that energy and raw material intelligence will become the basic technology of our century and that it will be closely linked with the expansion of renewable energy. It will become the stimulus for innovation and capital investment, following Nikolai Kondratiev's long wave theory. The theory states that prosperity and employment in an economy depend on long-term phases of the business cycle being recognized early on."

The theory which the minister is referring to posits that a basic innovation emerges every thirty to fifty years through which previously unknown, unused or unappreciated technologies gain significance. To date, five such waves and basic innovations have been identified: namely, the steam engine for the textile industry; steel for railways and transporting large amounts of people and goods by rail; electrical engineering and chemistry; petrochemistry in conjunction with the automobile; and information technology in conjunction with the computer which have brought us the internet and the cellphone since 1980.

The question is: what will stimulate the sixth wave? It is argued that we will recognize it in the form of dematerialization of the economy and prosperity. This has already begun. Other experts see the role of the current basic innovation more in the realm of health or education, but this need not contradict the idea of dematerialization.

No less than fifteen years ago, I called for the innovation of goods and services with the maximum possible resource productivity as an essential prerequisite for an ecologically sustainable economy.

In Japan, questions about the significance of MIPS and Factor 10 have been included in the list of questions for all university applicants since 2007.

Can designers, architects, design engineers, and bankers put us on the path towards the ecologically and economically decisive lightness of being? Towards a dematerialized service economy, an intelligent economy of moderation in which individual customers' desires are satisfied, with pleasure, with high quality, durability, and reasonably priced? By means of planned antiques, so to speak? Will we ever be able to achieve Factor 10?

Yes, we can, as hundreds of real-life examples show. Often, things even improve in quality, become more "modern" and more elegant, and have longer life spans. In addition, this development creates jobs! Wouldn't it be inspiring to work on developing and using everyday objects that begin to realize our dreams for a better future? For example, wouldn't it be very exciting to bring the ecological rucksack of the German health system down from the 4.5 metric tons of nature per capita per year, lowering the system's immense costs to a level that our grandchildren and their grandchildren will still be able to afford? Water use in the German paper industry, in any case, has dropped by a factor of six since 1960. A core paper manufacturer in Düsseldorf, Germany lowered its wastewater discharge from 260,000 m³ per year to zero, resulting in savings of 400,000 euros per year for wastewater charges. So the plant's MIPS for water was reduced to an infinitesimal amount.

The following is a cutting-edge example of how a man set out to realize his dream. Mankind has been using ships for transportation for more than 6000 years. The idea of using kites for propulsion is probably almost as old. Unlike sails, however, kites have never been a practical alternative to this day. The main reasons were inadequate materials and the difficulties in steering them. Merchant vessels burned fuel worth 25 billion euros in the year 2001. Fuel accounts for up to 60% of the total costs of running a ship, and that figure is increasing rapidly.

Stefan Wrage from Hamburg, Germany, knows his way around the shipping industry. Six years ago, the young engineer undertook to defy all previous experience. He had neither the money nor the support of ingenious engineers for the idea he believed in obsessively. "I'm going to build kites for cargo ships," he told me back then. Today, his staff numbers almost forty, he has reliable financing, and he has already been awarded half a dozen prizes for his work, among them one from the EXPO 05 in Japan.

He has named his product and his business "SkySails" (contact@skysails.de). For the most part, the technical problems have been solved, and Stefan Wrage sold his propulsion device for the first time in 2007. The kite is steered automatically and is safe to operate. Up to 60% of fuel costs can be saved, and no additional personnel are required on the vessel.

It is anything but common practice in Germany for a young inventor without financial resources to prevail despite the mistrust on the part of banks, "experts," and bureaucracy. But apparently, it is not entirely impossible even today in the land of the Siemenses, the Boschs, and the Zeppelins.

A Factor 10 improvement can seldom be accomplished by perfecting existing technologies. Attaching little machines to the backs of dinosaurs to consume the smoke they emit won't cut the mustard. We need to develop entirely new processes and facilities, entirely new products, and new forms of providing services that have been designed from the outset to minimize material flows. We must set an "eco-efficiency revolution" in motion. Or would it be better to speak of a "resource productivity revolution?" That would be an awful new coinage! However, the word "efficiency" is usually used to denote technical parameters for measuring the performance of an existing facility or of an existing process, while the term "productivity" also includes entirely new processes and goods that make the same service or a better one available. The productivity of the raw materials employed must increase dramatically, and that means that, regardless of which facilities or techniques we use, we must derive significantly more performance and prosperity from the same amount of raw materials. In the concept of the productivity revolution, the use of resources is linked to the (not only material) prosperity of a society.

Apparently, one of the most exciting tasks for engineers is to create "low MIPS" service machines that satisfy service expectations and make do with an average of about 10% of the customary amount of materials. Such measures towards savings (in other words, towards increasing resource productivity) can occur at any location during the goods' life cycle, that is, one can optimize at points during production, use, and disposal of products which are particularly advantageous both from a business perspective and from a technical point of view. We have discussed this question repeatedly with engineers in many sectors of manufacturing. We have debated with first-class designers and read the relevant literature. The responses are unequivocal: yes, it is indeed possible, but often does not pay off financially, at least not yet.

Making MIPS smaller: dematerializing existing products

After analyzing the shop from an ecological point of view and doing everything to reduce the day-to-day costs for energy, water, and material as far as possible, we will now get to work on the company's favorite product and streamline it ecologically, initially without changing its construction principle or its function.

1 Every assessment of a product's compatibility with the economy and its potential to damage the environment must include its entire life cycle, the analysis must cover everything "from the cradle back to the cradle."
2 The utility of processes, products, and services must be optimized.
3 The input of natural materials and energy per unit of service (MIPS) should be reduced by, on average, at least a factor of ten: resource productivity must be enhanced accordingly.
4 The use of land per unit of utility/service must be minimized.
5 Emissions and discharges of hazardous substances must be minimized.
6 Use of sustainably renewable resources should be maximized.

Our first step is to take a look at the rules above to gain an overview of the direction our work is to take. Now we get down to the nitty-gritty. Experience has shown that it is worth working through the following list together with the director of the company and all relevant staff (including representatives of the procurement and sales divisions). Once possibilities for dematerializing the selected reference product have been identified, the necessary capital investments and their amortization must be taken into consideration.

Key design properties for eco-design

Manufacturing
- material intensity (materials, processes)*
- energy intensity (materials, processes)*
- renewable resource inputs*
- useful material outputs*
- waste intensity *
- refusal rate*
- transport intensity*
- packaging intensity*
- hazardous materials

Use, Consumption
- material throughput*
- energy input*
- weight*
- self-monitoring, self-optimization*
- multi-functionality*
- potential for subsequent (different) uses*
- potential for joint use (for example, by several families)*
- size
- surface area needed
- dispersive hazardous material outputs
- longevity*
- availability of spare parts for extended time period*
- surface properties
- anti-corrosivity*
- repairability, exchangeability of parts*
- structure of the product and ease of disassembly*
- robustness, reliability*
- likelihood of material fatigue*
- adaptability to technical progress*

After first use
- low-MIPS collecting and sorting potentials*
- re-usability*
- usability for different purposes*
- re-manufacturing potential for same use*
- material composition and complexity (ease of recycling for chemical/metal-lurgical reasons)*
- recycling potential of parts and materials for same or other uses*

Disposal
- combustion potential (usable energy outputs)*
- potential for composting
- impacts on environment after disposal

                                              * = included in MIPS computations

Designing the invisible: innovations for tomorrow

Economically and ecologically modern design begins, without exception, with as precise a description as possible of the utility which people expect from a product, or which they do not expect or would even like to avoid. For this purpose, their needs, desires, and dreams must first of all be known. In order to really know about needs, one must talk with people extensively and specifically; for instance with one's partners and children, and with friends and acquaintances over a beer or at the sports club. Current-day marketing studies hardly provide answers. If we define the purpose, the desired utility, or the anticipated bundle of utility before technologies are designed – in other words, if we do not merely dematerialize existing types of products – then we can reach entirely new and highly dematerialized solutions for fulfilling needs. For example, the Technical University of Vienna built a house near St. Pölten in Austria with 300 square meters of floor space and achieved resource productivity ten times greater than usual. The heating needs are met with the heat loss of the computers used in the house!

We should not seek a better window cleaning agent, but rather a way of cleaning glass and other surfaces or even preventing them from getting dirty in the first place, a possibility that saves resources and energy. This vantage point permits us to develop novel, unusual ideas that reduce the consumption of nature in comparison with traditional solutions system-wide.

This is a tall order for a normal small business that produces window cleaning agents. Which of the few staff members, who already have their hands full helping the business turn a profit, should take the time to think far beyond the competences of their employer? And even if an idea for a completely new technical solution for "keeping windows clean" were to be born within

Eco-intelligent (eco-efficient) goods are objects, tools, machines, vehicles, buildings, and infrastructures that provide maximum utility (and different kinds of utility, measured against the individual customer's needs) at market prices and minimize material, energy, waste, transportation, packaging, dangerous substances, and use of surface area during the entire life cycle – from raw material extraction to recycling – for as long a period as possible.

the company, would the necessary resources – including time – be available to enter into the risk of new development? Many an owner of a small business has tried and succeeded, and names such as Diesel, Lilienthal, and Benz remind us of this fact. With the advent of the internet, the chances of being successful should be greatly enhanced. However, many were and are driven out of business due to such attempts.

Inventing new technical solutions to create utility means reducing the ecological rucksacks of all the material goods involved. Since ecological rucksacks are invisible, we apparently need to learn *how to design the invisible*. That is new and exciting for designers, architects, and engineers. Yet it does not correspond in the slightest with their self-image as individuals who create new things that people can touch and use.

In short: as much utility as possible for less nature and less money. Even when we design service machines, strategies such as possibilities for multiple uses or joint use, use in succession, renting goods, or offering services must be taken into consideration, too. Thinking in systems is of substantial importance for the designer and engineer of the future.

Designers have many more opportunities to influence the resource intensity of the service providing machines right from the beginning when it comes to mass and energy flows – much more than regarding (potentially) toxic materials. Indeed, there are no limits to ingenuity for paving the many ways to sustainability, as everyone can think about how to improve MIPS, be it for existing solutions, or with the aid of radically new ideas.

Real market competition is thus integrated in the creation of ecologically better goods and services – meaningful competition that will also pay off correspondingly on the market. The Japanese understood this long ago: in the year 2001, Factor 10 was integrated into national strategic economic planning – the reason why Ernst Ulrich von Weizsäcker and I were honored with the World Environment Award at that time.

Multifunctional equipment

Multifunctional equipment such as the Swiss army knife, certain robots, kitchen appliances, and computers, can carry out different tasks and services, and therefore also create different types of utility. From an ecological point of view, this is useful, because MIPS is smaller for each of the possible services than it would be if many individual pieces of equipment had to be used.

Of course some appliances have many more built-in functions than a normal customer – such as you or I – need. Did a manufacturer or its representative ever ask you what you want? I, for one, have never been approached. Braun Design once invented a bracket that can be mounted to cover the knobs and buttons on a washing machine in order to reduce the seventy-five built-in combinations of functions to a handful, making it

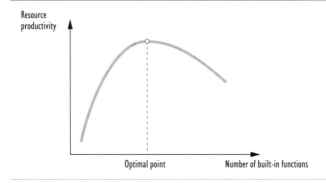

Figure 16 While building different functions into a piece of equipment
can have a positive effect on the resource productivity of
individual functions at first (Swiss army knife), overloading a
piece of equipment with different functions can decrease
productivity (e.g. robustness of equipment and its longevity
decline) – and can frustrate users because of increasingly
complex operation

more human and – as was believed – more ecological to operate
the machine.

In any case, equipping tools and appliances with additional
functions requires resources, increases the complexity of operating and repairing them as well as their sensitivity, which can also
cause early failure and therefore necessitate replacement. Fig. 16
shows how the advantages of multifunctional pieces of equipment can backfire.

Designing sustainable utility

Using the Factor 10/MIPS concept is not tied to certain technologies ("there is no technical fix"). It should be taken for granted

that tried and true technologies and manufacturing processes will be employed.

MIPS always refers to the usable product. For example, the statement that a house is equipped with an exemplary dematerialized heating system is only one aspect out of many when it comes to increasing resource productivity of the service "housing." And still, and it cannot be emphasized often enough: without taking all aspects – from the cradle to the grave – into account and dematerializing them, we will not be able to make the leap to a future with a future. The freedom for all to participate in improving the entire economic system, its technologies, and the utility provided, knows no bounds.

Let us sum up a few facts and circumstances from which we must draw logical conclusions: Realizing a sustainable future requires that economic, social, and ecological goals be interlinked. There are no decisions which do not also affect the ecosphere, be they in the political, economic, or private realm. An economy that does not save resources in a targeted fashion is not sustainable. Solutions to problems will pave the way towards sustainability in the future if they focus on the utility of things. True innovation does not mean increasing the number of things available by new means, but rather creating quality of life with less resource use. Such products will almost certainly be especially successful on the world's markets in the future.

A sustainable solution to the plight of the environment must begin at the input side of the economy, and must help to design all products, services, and processes more ecologically. It must be cost-efficient and must utilize market forces to provide financial rewards for the ecologically better option. Global social justice requires respect for the dignity and the needs of all people, and means advocating that everyone have sufficient access to the resources of the Earth, the only planet on which we can live.

Germany would have to be much larger than it is to produce all the things that the Germans consume. The way things are, however, the Germans simply use the land area of other countries.

Other rich nations act in a similar fashion. In this way, we human beings are in the process of endangering the habitability of the only planet available to us. We often force new conditions on the ecosphere without knowing whether the services of nature will sustain the impacts.

It is high time to eliminate the systemic root cause for the incompatibility between today's economic activities and the continued functioning of the life-sustaining services of nature, without which humans cannot survive. For survival on planet Earth, the time has come to implement damage-preventing strategies. The Earth is in our hands.

There are steps we can take today, immediately. We do not have as much time as we might want. Since it takes ten to twenty years to develop sweeping technical changes and for them to penetrate the market, we must live with the fact that effective dematerialization will take decades. And since every peaceful social change takes a generation or longer, a realistic timeframe for establishing the sustainable development of the economy would be twenty to forty years. In other words, there is time – but it is time to act.

The productivity of labor and resources

Even the longest journey begins with the first step. Let us attempt to take such a step by examining the productivity of labor and resources. Apparently, the prices of materials rarely induce businesses nowadays to seek new ways to lower costs. This is astounding, because, according to the German Federal Statistical Office, the average costs for the factors of material and energy are greater than 50%, while average costs for labor make up 22%. For many years, however, firms have been pursuing ways to improve the productivity of labor – that is, improving the use of paid labor to produce salable products.

However, since people quickly reach their natural limits of working more rapidly and more efficiently – that is, making shoes by hand faster and faster, hammering nails more and more efficiently, or shoveling out coal more and more quickly – entrepreneurs began early on to introduce technical innovations to solve this dilemma: new tools, machines, and equipment.

Over the course of time, machines replacing human labor became ever more efficient and intelligent, right up to robots. A modern machine can mine as much lignite as approximately 25,000 workers by hand. Productivity of labor – in fact, productivity of machinery – was increased by a factor of about fifty in the course of a century.

At the same time, the ecological rucksacks of machines became ever heavier, and more and more of them were brought into operation in more and more companies. In other words, the process of liberating man from work with the help of machines was supported by subsidies from the ecosphere. The efficiency, comfort, and safety of work achieved in this way were attained increasingly at the expense of ecological stability.

The events of the past hundred years are reminiscent of a spiral: entrepreneurs first hired more workers to increase their incomes (from production). The workers demanded and received higher wages (shares of profits) with the support of their trade unions. Thus, the cost of labor went up, and so did the cost of living, of course, even if more slowly than wage increases. That is why the "standard of living" rose. Under the pressure of competition and eager to make more and more profits – allegedly an innate human instinct – entrepreneurs increasingly sought to use machines as substitutes for human labor. The (remaining) employees still received shares of the higher profits. Meanwhile,

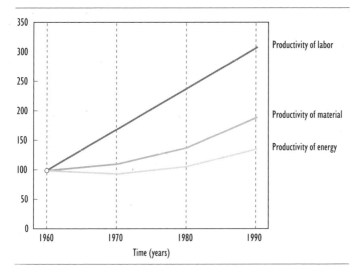

Figure 17 The development of the productivity of energy, material, and labor in West Germany since 1960

unemployment became more frequent and pervasive – and nature paid for it.

What makes things more difficult is that the government traditionally finances a considerable part of its expenditures by taxing profits as well as incomes from labor. Unfortunately, nobody has ever been able to explain to me why active commitment to creating quality of life, contentment, happiness, and joy are punished by being taxed.

This peculiar practice on the part of the public authorities to take in such monies fuels the spiral even more, particularly as the revenues from income taxes are used to finance many of the government's various social obligations, for example unemployment benefits, pensions, etc. The results: increasing unemployment, increasing governmental budgetary problems, and increasing consumption of nature.

Since the 1970s, we have found ourselves in a situation in which we actually do produce and export more and more, but without it helping us to attain more prosperity and quality of life domestically. In the words of Franz Lehner, the President of the Institute for Work and Technology in Gelsenkirchen, Germany, "Real incomes and other important indicators for prosperity and quality of life have been stagnating for many years, or are even declining. What is more: the prosperity gained so far is called into question again and again by strategies to secure competitiveness and by attempts to cope with global structural change which are not particularly innovative."

Unemployment with no prospects?

As we have already seen, an economy is sustainable if it harmonizes the three dimensions of social affairs, economic affairs, and the preservation of the services of nature with one another. An economy is sustainable if it is capable of increasing utility for all, at the same time securing the natural, social, and economic foundations for the future on which this capability depends. Unemployment is a question of social justice. High unemployment means not having the social dimension of sustainability under control.

Unemployment is a consequence of adhering to outdated structures of taxation and to concepts of (re)distribution from a time when endless growth seemed possible. It is a consequence of a lack of flexibility and a lack of innovations, especially in the fields of resource productivity, finance, education, research priorities, and management.

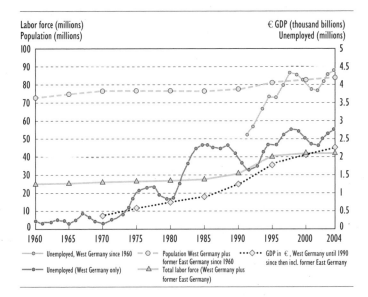

Figure 18 Trends in Germany since 1960 for population growth, labor force size, unemployment, and volume of production (GDP)

Total population and persons employed are shown for West Germany and former East Germany together. In 1998, the population in West Germany was approximately 63 million, that of former East Germany approximately 16 million. The GDP shown is that of West Germany alone until 1990, thereafter combined with that of former East Germany. Unemployment figures are shown for West Germany from 1960 to 2004, and for West Germany and former East Germany combined since 1990 as a separate curve. In West Germany, unemployment tended to increase stepwise since 1960 during times of recessions, declining somewhat during times when business picked up, and rising again thereafter in absolute numbers. (Data kindly provided by Prof. Harry Lehmann.)

It is a unanimous insight in the business and political communities that none of the favorable phases of the business cycle since the mid-1970s have been used to take a good, hard look at foreseeable problems with insuring the population in Germany against all possible risks and to push through the consequences in a timely manner. "Health insurance costs will decline," we heard, "Pensions are secure," or "Long-term care insurance has a sustainable financial base" and the like, even striking predictions by two Federal Chancellors, "We will cut unemployment in half."

Let us take a look at how unemployment has developed in recent decades.

Since 1960, unemployment in (West) Germany has been increasing relentlessly, step by step to ever higher levels. The steps are marked by periods of economic recovery, in other words, by a certain easing of tensions on the labor market. These positive phases were followed by increasing losses of paid labor and so on and so forth, until today (see Fig. 18). From this perspective, a significant decrease in unemployment is not to be expected without a paradigm shift in the framework conditions of the German economy. In Germany, labor costs on average more than twice as much as people receive for their actual work. The remainder is claimed by the public authorities to pay for their tasks and the ever-growing interest on their unfunded expenditures and debts. Is this necessary? Is it socially responsible? Is it just? But above all: is it intelligent and sustainable?

Misdirected financial burdens?

Citizens and the business community complain about the tax burden, about health, unemployment, and pension insurance. They all rely overwhelmingly on one factor of production: labor. The demographic development will further exacerbate this problem. The goal should be to lower the unemployment rate to distinctly less than 5%. That sounds ambitious – but it can be done. Other countries have achieved it already, for example, Japan, the Netherlands, and Austria.

In recent years, many new jobs have been created in Germany, but not enough. Even if this trend should stabilize in the medium term, unemployment will hardly decline permanently. Additional jobs will fall victim to continued structural change. New jobs – above all ones with high value creation – are needed.

Traditional economic doctrine holds that at least 3% growth per year over the next ten years would be necessary in order to create three to four million additional jobs in Germany. The target for growth would be lower, however, if we were to succeed in creating growth in areas that require more labor and less resource use. In plain language, that means that resource productivity should be increased to ease the situation in the labor market.

Germany must readjust its fiscal system if the country is to make decisive progress in reducing unemployment. Revenues, expenditures, and subsidies must be shifted towards heightened resource efficiency. The long-term goal is to achieve a balanced and economically sensible burden on all the factors of production: labor, capital, and energy/resources. Innovative models for full-time and part-time work and a more flexible labor market will contribute to making this succeed as well.

Energy and resource efficiency

In spite of relatively low costs for natural resources, energy and resource-efficient sectors have a strong tradition in Germany. Better-insulated homes, more efficient motors, better technology, all this is already having an effect. Energy efficiency has improved markedly in recent years. Intelligent use of resources works in a similar way. Whether we are looking at housing, clothing, transport, information, or entertainment, the basic rule is that achieving the same level of comfort with less consumption of nature is feasible. For the economy, it means deriving greater value creation from a given amount of material or energy. The result is a double dividend, economic and ecological, in other words: a *win-win* situation taking us towards sustainability.

From 1960 to 1990, productivity of labor increased by approximately 3.8% per year in Germany. National total material flow (TMF) increased by 1.6% during the same period, while the gross domestic product grew by 3.1%. Apparently, there was a distinct decoupling of the German economy from resource consumption. It is notable, however, that the absolute consumption of natural resources did *not* decrease, as approaching sustainability demands. This points to the fact that we should be cautious in using relative indicators.

Increases in the productivity of labor gain greater media attention because they are often the reason why workers are laid off. Improvements in resource productivity, on the other hand, usually take place without much commotion. One reason for this may be that politicians, the media, and the public are still not fully aware of how resource productivity is connected to reaching economic and ecological sustainability. Another reason may be that increasing resource productivity in the production sector is frequently the result of focused innovation and may not be divulged publicly.

Unintelligent taxation

The current system of taxes and duties guides economic activity in the wrong direction. It distributes burdens inefficiently and unfairly. Because of the structure of taxes and charges (among other reasons), the current cost structure of production looks like this: 70% for labor, 25% for capital, and just 5 percent for energy. An entirely different picture emerges if we ask: how high are the payments for the end result – material value creation – in reality? Empirical studies in the US, Japan, and Germany have shown that value creation in industry changes just as much due to a change in energy input as it does when labor and capital inputs together change by a total of 1%. In other words, labor is more expensive in relation to its contribution to output. Energy, in contrast, contributes relatively more to value creation, but costs comparatively little.

Under these circumstances, rationalizing production means cutting jobs! Not least, and above all, because social welfare systems today depend almost entirely on labor. The labor market is decoupled from economic growth. The consequences are declining tax revenues and increasing social expenditures. The government operates in a vicious circle, with less and less room to maneuver for expenditures towards prevention and sustainability.

For this reason, it is necessary to readjust the optimal point when determining resource use. The economically rational mix for the input of labor, capital, and material/energy must be shifted towards more labor and less material and energy use.

Governments set the rules under which business and the market operate. And only government can adjust the economic and fiscal framework conditions for improving the chances to move toward sustainability.

Ensuring credibility and public acceptance for such shifts demands as a minimum cost-neutrality and sufficient transparency.

Full-cost pricing

The signals and incentives that individual people as well as businesses receive from the market decide production and consumption. In a market economy, the most important and predominant signal is the price. Nowadays, most energy and commodity prices are distorted by government interventions in the markets. Taxes and fiscal incentives, price fixing and market policies, exchange rates and trade barriers all influence the energy and resource intensity of growth, and the extent to which growth harms the services of nature.

Without regard to the facts, most governments, entrepreneurs, and voters continue to assume that an economy is healthy if the consumption of energy, materials, and resources is on the increase in order to create more goods, jobs, and income. This assumption is a leftover of an economy based on mass production, the economy of an epoch reaching its end, in which growth was characterized by the constant expansion of energy provision, the exploitation of resources, and environmental devastation. Even though these assumptions are long a thing of the past, they continue to dominate in finance, energy, agricultural, forestry, and other policies. The consequence is that the development towards a new, efficient, and sustainable economy is slowed down, in part even blocked.

These misguided assumptions also dominate environmental policy, which continues to concentrate on the output side of the economy rather than on the entire system. End-of-pipe solutions and resource processing or recycling tend to get more support than productivity increases. This leads to a constant increase in the costs of environmental protection.

The reality of wasting resources

Practical experience in hundreds of small and medium-sized enterprises in Europe shows that considerable potentials for saving energy and material are not utilized. On average, the saving potentials are between 20 to 25%, whereby the capital investments that are sometimes necessary would pay for themselves in less than two years. In some enterprises, the potentials for savings are even considerably higher.

Of course, these observations raise the question: is this a case of market failure? Why are the efforts to save resource costs not as intense as possible? Why does cost pressure almost always result in workers losing their jobs, but only rarely in savings of kilowatt-hours or cement?

The reasons for this situation have often been pondered. The following are probably among the most important ones: many managers in small and medium-sized enterprises are not familiar enough with thinking in systems. They are rarely interested in thinking through the history of their products "from the cradle to the grave." When they make decisions, the decisive factors are the costs within the company for capital, labor, and intermediate products as well as the profits the business can make. Resource flows, measured in units of weight, and the resource intensity of their products are not part of most book-keeping systems.

Apparently, the concepts of the ecological rucksack and MIPS are not yet sufficiently widespread. And since the purchase prices of intermediate products, raw materials, and supplies do not reflect their resource efficiency ("do not tell the ecological truth"), most entrepreneurs do not know the amount of nature that has already been consumed when they purchase inputs, transform them into their products, and finally market them. Small businesses may also be hesitant about experimenting with alternative processes, new materials, and new product design. Norms and standards often make innovation difficult, for example in the food packaging industry and the construction sector.

In the final analysis we must also ask: is advertising on the wrong track? How many customers are really interested in resource productivity and its significance for the future?

Innovation on the wrong track?

In March 2006, the German parliament, the *Bundestag*, voted to add 25 billion euros to the budget. A considerable part of these funds were to benefit research leading to more innovation. Now, Germany is one of the three top countries in the European Union when it comes to the number of patent applications per capita. That is good news, because patents are not possible without innovation, and innovation is, as it were, part of the capital necessary to compete with other countries at the vanguard of technology.

From time immemorial, politics and societal priorities have influenced the focal points of innovation. They follow a society's taboos, fears, and hopes; they mirror its customs, and change only hesitantly – unless life-threatening circumstances force new solutions. The reader will be aware – at the latest since the discussion about genetically modified organisms – that there are also bans on research directed at innovation.

I wondered to which extent today's innovations might reveal a trend towards a future with a future.

Figure 19 shows what I found. When supplementing the EU correlation between innovation and patent applications in industrialized countries with the correlation of patent applications and annual per capita consumption of non-renewable resources

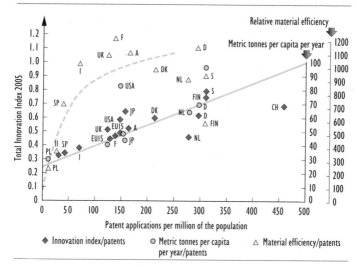

Figure 19   The solid line sloping upwards from left to right shows the
correlation between the total innovation index (y-axis) and
the number of patent applications per million of the
population (x-axis) for Member States of the European Union
(EU 25) as well as the United States, Japan, Norway, and
Switzerland

This trend is virtually identical for the consumption of non-renewable natural
resources per person-year in the countries listed, indicating that the innovation
strength of a country does *not* translate into a slowdown in the consumption of
nature. (Innovation data from Eurostat).

in the countries affected (Table 4), a practically identical straight
line result, sloping upwards to the right.

Apparently, the amount of natural resource consumption
follows the power to innovate exactly: the more patent applications, the more consumption of nature per capita in these
countries!

The result seems paradoxical. One could conclude cynically

that the *fewer* innovations today, the better for the ecosphere. But in reality, present-day innovations obviously have entirely different goals from sustainability. We would surely not be surprised to learn that innovations today are still primarily geared towards improving the productivity of labor (i.e. of machines).

If we also graph the material efficiency in the affected countries against their annual patent applications, we get the curve shown in the figure, sloping upwards from the lower left-hand side (dotted line).

I believe it would be worth the effort of good statisticians to analyze these correlations more closely.

Quite obviously, when providing financial support for innovation toward a certain end, defining the boundary conditions precisely is of great importance.

For me, eco-innovation means the creation of novel and competitively priced goods, processes, systems, services, and procedures that can satisfy human needs and bring quality of life to all people with life-cycle-wide minimal use of natural resources (material including energy carriers and surface area) per unit of output, and a minimal release of toxic substances. (Since adopted by the EU, see EUROPE INNOVA, Final Report for Sectoral Innovation Watch, May 2008)

Only businesses that are proactive and have demonstrable successes in this field should consider themselves part of eco-industry.

The Aachen scenario

During the last fifteen years and more, Ernst Ulrich von Weizsäcker, myself, and others have undauntedly promoted the idea of shifting the overhead on wages from labor to natural resources, thereby creating economic incentives for innovations towards sustainability.

Moreover, practical discussions in far more than 100 small and medium-sized enterprises had convinced us that on average, at least 20% of the expenditures on resources were unnecessary in order to market the results of the company's work.

The former Finance Minister of Greece and Environmental Commissioner in Brussels Yannis Paleocrassas elaborated that such a radical reorientation is not just an unrealistic dream as early as 1999 in a piece he authored for the International Factor 10 Club. Supported financially by the private Aachen Foundation, Professor Bernd Meyer (author of *Costing the Earth: Perspectives on Sustainable Development* in this series) and his colleagues at the University of Osnabrück, Germany, have undertaken simulation studies in the last three years with the goal of tracking down the economic consequences of saving 20% of resource costs in Germany. For these studies, Meyer used his model Inforge in combination with the model Panta Rhei. Stefan Bringezu of the Wuppertal Institute provided the necessary data on Total Material Flow. Above all, the research focused on the question how this development might affect the competitiveness of the German economy, the creation of new jobs, and the development of the national budget. The results have been published and are known as the Aachen Scenario.

In a next step, Meyer broadened the study by asking the question: what would be the additional effects of establishing a progressive material input tax in place of income taxation in a cost-neutral way? The 20% resource input cost savings were assumed to be realized between 2006 and 2016, and the tax shifting option was assumed for the years from 2011 to 2020. The simulated tax shift was set at 1 euro per metric ton per year for material input, and income tax was assumed to be lowered by the same amount (16 billion euros in 2016, or approximately 10% of income tax revenue in 2001). This simulation did not take energy carriers and water into account.

The results point towards an increase in gross domestic product (GDP) of greater than 1 percent, and in addition a continual stabilization of the national budget with additional revenue of 80 billion euros per year in 2016, and savings of 160 billion euros for industry. In addition, we can count on the creation of more than one million new jobs, and a distinct trend towards the service sector. The resulting dematerialization was calculated at 18%.

Meyer's results apparently exceed by far all other options for improving Germany's economic situation that are currently being debated. Meyer also studied the question of which of Germany's fifty-nine statistical economic sectors could contribute most to the expected dematerialization. To do so, he simulated the response to a minor reduction of resources in all sectors. The fifty-nine sectors are characterized by approximately 3500 separate resource links.

The surprising result was that 50% of all possible savings could be attained along just sixteen of these links, and that forty links were responsible for almost 100% of the simulated dematerializations. These differences are evidently of considerable practical significance for the rational design of taxation shifts.

We still lack information

It seems to me that the surprisingly positive macroeconomic results of the above-mentioned simulations should encourage further studies with substantially more breadth and depth. They should be financed at least in part with public funding.

From my point of view, larger studies should examine the consequences of substantially larger tax shifts than Meyer has been able to study to date. Water and energy carriers should be included in the simulations as well. In Germany, water consumption amounts to approximately 500 metric tons per capita per year, 70% of which are in the agricultural sector. Water supply in Germany is largely under national control and is subject to extensive metering of the quantities consumed. In addition to the forty linkages mentioned above that are responsible for large segments of the economic metabolism, the ecological rucksacks of natural resources should possibly also be taxed.

Carnoules Potentials

There are a number of further options for promoting the improvement of resource productivity. They are sometimes called "Carnoules Potentials" and include the following:

1 Reorientation of private and public priorities for research and development so that they benefit the creation of social, institutional, ecological, and economic innovations with the goal of saving natural resources. In my opinion, there is still too much emphasis on developing technologies that enhance the productivity of labor, including robotics.

2 Establishment of a publicly accessible institution to elaborate, continually update, and make available information and data that serve to improve resource productivity, including ecological rucksacks, MIF, MIPS, TMF, etc. Such an institution could also monitor transparent labeling of goods and services.

3 Development and rapid introduction of curricula and

courses on the theoretical understanding of resource productivity in all fields, as well as its practical improvement throughout its life-cycle, including indicators and methodologies for measurement. This applies to all fields and levels of education.

4 Routine dissemination in the mass media of current data and information about the development of resource productivity at the national and global levels in various sectors of the economy as well as best-practice examples of products, vehicles, buildings, infrastructures, and services.

5 In addition to the already existing awards for special achievements in dematerializing systems, goods, and services, highly-endowed (up to one million euros) international prizes could be announced and awarded every year.

6 Review of all German and European Union norms and standards regarding the resource flows they cause, as well as their readjustment, where appropriate.

7 Rapid and sharp reduction of all subsidies that contribute to resource consumption.

8 Taxation of all businesses and individuals that have free access to resource extraction from nature.

9 Creation of incentives for offering products with very long warranties, for the transition from selling products to leasing arrangements, and for offering more services.

10 Public procurement regulations that give preference to products and services with high resource productivity.

11 Taxing advertisements that encourage consumption, make exaggerated or misleading claims, and/or extol the ecological virtues of activities at the rate of 1%. The revenues should be used for correcting and supplementing the contents of the advertisement with a view toward its

contribution to approaching sustainability, and in particular to improving resource productivity.

Investing in tomorrow

If prices do not tell the ecological truth, what about profits? Up to now, they usually don't! In the long term, this could turn out to be a risk for profits, and therefore also for the financial markets as a whole. If investors routinely regarded profits in conjunction with sustainable business management, then surely portfolio risk management would be quite different in the future than what we know today.

One task of the financial markets is to anticipate future risks and include them in investment decisions. Accordingly, one of the central questions is: what is a fair price for an investment if ecological risks are taken into account? From the perspective of the MIPS concept, the answer seems clear: the higher the resource productivity of functionally equivalent products, and the smaller their ecological rucksacks, the more sustainable the producer's operation is. Unfortunately, however, the amount of data required for this index is not available as yet. But investments should be made in as forward-looking a way as possible. What is to be done?

Most investors have come to understand that climate change and its risks are a reality. Consumption of fossil energy carriers in Germany – a metric for CO_2 emissions – account for no less than 10% of the resources used for economic purposes. And CO_2 is linked to most products' final use due to their fossil energy consumption, often in the form of electricity.

Therefore, it seems reasonable that the financial markets might attempt to anticipate the risks linked to climate change in order to estimate "fairer" prices. It may be surprising, but some actors are in fact trying to do so already.

The Sustainable Asset Management (SAM) group in Zurich can point to good results. Cooperating with Dow Jones Indexes, Alois Flatz at SAM developed the first ever "Sustainability Index", the "Dow Jones Sustainability Index" (DJSI). It measures the performance of the best 10 percent of businesses worldwide with respect to their CO_2 emissions. Within the framework of analysis for the DJSI, the CO_2 emissions of 300 globally leading businesses were identified. This data is increasingly being used by other actors on Wall Street, in addition to financial metrics, to draw initial conclusions about the environmental risks associated with investments.

The results so far are promising. Most investment products that integrate the sustainability aspect of CO_2 emissions outperformed the traditional products. For instance, the DJSI beat its benchmark, the MSCI (an index prepared by Morgan Stanley Capital International), by 19% since the calculations began in 1994.

Before a product-specific resource intensity analysis becomes possible, a next step towards improving the "Sustainability Index" could be accounting for businesses' material input per unit of turnover and/or per number of employees. The ecological rucksacks of the material inputs would have to be included in the calculations to improve differentiation between businesses. Otherwise, the manufacturers of information and communication technologies, or also realtors, for example, would appear in a much better light than the "ecological truth" would warrant.

Europe's historic opportunity

At the end of this book, I shall venture to write down my greatest dream. The most significant challenge of the 21st century is to provide well-being and dignity in security for a still growing world population. Sustainable well-being is possible only with sufficient availability and access to natural resources, with social peace, and in economically appropriate circumstances. Development to this end requires comprehensive eco-innovations. It is mankind's greatest investment opportunity.

While a relatively small number of people have more than enough natural resources at their disposal, billions of others require additional resources if they are to satisfy even their basic needs and maintain their human dignity in the future. At the same time, however, planet Earth is now already overextended. Soil erosion, loss of species, climate change, extreme weather events, water scarcity on all continents, scarcities of metals, fossil carbon, and carbohydrates from the seas are some of the consequences which can be measured even today.

But this is by no means only about the environment: in the medium and long term, the most important contribution to securing the supply of raw materials for the economy is using natural resources sparingly. Maximum possible resource productivity is what is needed from an economic, social, and ecological point of view, but also in light of international responsibility for peace and security.

The economy must be decoupled from natural resource consumption as much as technically possible, and to a far greater extent and far more rapidly than has occurred to date if we desire to secure our chances of having a future with a future. And wherever possible, this should take place without endangering the level of well-being which has already been attained.

The Lisbon Strategy of the European Union and the EU's Sustainable Development Strategy have already pointed out the key role of efficient resource use for worldwide economic development and have emphasized that the EU must take on a role of international leadership. The President of the European Commission, Jose Manuel Barroso, said recently, "Making the EU the most energy and resource efficient region in the world will drive forward innovation, create jobs, increase competitiveness and improve the state of the environment."

Holistic policy is essential if we wish to generate sustainable prosperity, well-being, and human dignity in security. The contours of how the concerns of the different dimensions of sustainability can be brought together in practice, and how they are to result in decisions, are not yet discernible in the political arena. The course towards the future has not been set reliably, neither in terms of content nor in terms of institutional framework. Issues falling under the aegis of the government departments for economic affairs, social affairs, consumption, research, technology, finance, justice, development, internal affairs, environmental protection, and others are often affected at the same time and to the same degree when it comes to formulating sustainable decisions. In the final analysis, only the head of state can take on responsibility for them.

Sustainability means dealing with today's challenges today – be they in the realms of the economy, ecology, or social matters – and not shifting them to future generations. To date, we have not succeeded in creating unified, harmonized policies that are viable for the future.

The memories of the many wars fought in Europe and the devastation they caused seem to have been blown away. A unified and peaceful Europe seems to be taken for granted by the younger generations, and accordingly appears not to require any particular efforts or commitment concerning strategic decisions for the future.

We should consider the failure of the European constitution and the oddly cool attitude many people have towards Europe as a mandate to venture upon a strategy for future viability and sustainability, to invest in Europe's future with the goal of giving global sustainability its possibly last chance.

Europe's new and epochal challenge is to conceive of an eco-social market economy and to make it come to life. A system that employs market forces in a socially responsible way would make sustainability possible in a free and peaceful world, and its success could serve as an example for others. Not a strategy of asceticism, coercion, or arrogance, but a trajectory that enables all those who use nature's treasures sparingly to benefit, guided by their own individual responsibility. A path that protects life, well-being, and human dignity and provides security, as well as happiness and jobs for all. Of course, freedom of speech and justice for all, as well as renunciation of violence are character-istics of such a future, too. Everyone should feel called upon to make a voluntary commitment to these goals. The relevance, transparency, and long-term reliability on the part of govern-ments and the economy will be measured against these goals.

Europe can look back on enough positive and negative his-torical experiences to move forward successfully on this path. Europe is strong enough economically to make a convincing case at the global level. And nobody will doubt that the continent's cultural, economic, and technical achievements provide the best possible foundation for a future with a future.

Active support of this strategy from all European Union Member States – as helpful as it might be – is not necessar-ily required at first. Every economically strong coalition from Europe – even including Norway and Switzerland – can promote this strategy on the political level with just as much determination as the US has displayed in fighting terrorist attacks around the globe.

As the EU's largest economic power, Germany should take the decisive steps as soon as at all possible – especially since Finland has already undertaken an initiative of this kind. During its EU Presidency, Finland presented a draft resolution that included the following at a meeting of the EU Environment Ministers in Turku, Finland from July 14 to 16, 2006: "The aim in the future should be to break the direct linkage between economic growth and the negative impacts of resource use on climate, biodiversity and ecosystems. This will be done by setting clear evidence-based targets and by using various practical instruments. Such a vision should look beyond traditional policymaking practices." The action plan presented mentions the enormous potential for dematerializing production and consumption, but also states that this would fall short by far if the goal is to make our current throughput economy sustainable. In addition, we need life-cycle-wide approaches. The draft resolution explicitly emphasizes that maintaining the services of the ecosphere, such as clean air and pure water, must be integrated in all policy fields as a key element of a new understanding of environmental policy (see "Going global on eco-efficiency – Finland's initiative towards a new generation of environmental policy" at www.ymparisto.fi).

Given current economic and environmental policies, nature's life-sustaining services will continue to decline at a rapid pace. "Business as usual" may put human life on Earth into question eventually. Meanwhile, economic options will become limited and world peace more fragile.

Traditional *environmental* policies focus on dealing with specific problems. In certain respects, this approach has been quite successful. For instance, it has cleaned up water pollution, taken dangerous products off the market, recycled certain products, and slowed the acceleration of climatic change.

However, since traditional problem solving begins *after* recognizing a problem's existence, such policies are neither helpful on a systems level, nor are they preventive in a general sense. Solving individual problems can even exacerbate other problems, in particular those as yet undiscovered.

"*Internalization of the environmental costs*" of individual known problems among millions of possible destructive interactions between hundreds of thousands of different pollutants and the highly complex ecosphere *cannot* be relied upon when seeking sustainable solutions.

Lately, *recycling* appears to be experiencing a policy revival

– except that its administrators and practitioners now call it "resources policy." While recycling can contribute toward saving natural resources, there is no evidence that this "end-of-the-pipe" approach could ever lead to sustainable conditions. Much of the damage to the services of nature has been done *before* waste treatment can begin. Typically, national recycling policies can cover only a few percent of total materials flows. In Germany, about 1 or 2% of the total resource flow is recycled today – at a yearly expense of several billion euros.

Today, more than 95% of the resources lifted from nature are wasted before the finished goods reach the market. And many industrial products – such as cars – demand additional natural resources while being used.

It is high time to eliminate the *systemic root cause* for the incompatibility between today's economic activities and the continued functioning of the life-sustaining services of nature without which humans cannot survive. For survival on planet Earth, it is high time to implement truly *damage-preventing strategies*.

Today, the *fundamental physical flaw* of human activities is the enormous consumption of natural resources per unit of output of value or service. This observation applies to all renewable and nonrenewable materials, domestic animals, diversity of species, water, soil, and land use.

The key to sustainability is to radically increase the resource productivity of all economic activities, including energy generation.

While it may seem obvious, it is nevertheless worth repeating that climatic change, too, is the consequence of enormous flows of human-induced carbonaceous material, and of large quantities of N_2O emissions, originating from the technical fixation of millions of tons of nitrogen from the air for producing fertilizer.

Since the mid-1990s, it has been widely accepted that to be successful in approaching sustainability, an average *minimum tenfold dematerialization* of the western lifestyle in absolute terms has to be achieved. "Factor 4" was suggested later, but cannot satisfy sustainable conditions.

Today, the environmental safety threshold has already been surpassed, as is evident from such developments as climatic change, widespread hunger and water shortages, desertification, the spread of diseases, massive erosion, and increasing natural catastrophes such as hurricanes and floods. And yet, only some 20% of humankind enjoys the full benefits of our economic model, while *all* human beings – and in particular the poor – have begun to suffer the consequences of its flaws.

But even if one were to ignore the ecological problems caused by the overuse of nature, globalizing the western lifestyle is *not* possible because it would require more than two planets as a resource basis. Rapidly rising raw material prices testify to this.

Technologies for tomorrow

To translate the findings just outlined into a general guideline for policy development, the European Union's Panel on Eco-Innovation recently concluded*:

> Eco-Innovation means the creation of novel and competitively
> priced goods, processes, systems, services, and procedures that
> can satisfy human needs and bring quality of life to all people
> with a life-cycle-wide minimal use of natural resources (material
> including energy carriers, and surface area) per unit output, and
> a minimal release of toxic substances.

---

* See Chapter 7 of this book, and EUROPE INNOVA SYSTEMATIC, technopolis group, "Eco-Innovation," Final Report, 2008

This suggests that continued reliance on traditional *"environmental technologies"* is no longer enough. Many examples exist where incremental improvement of existing technologies has increased resource productivity two to four times. However, sufficiently decoupling production and consumption from nature requires new systems, goods, services, processes, and procedures for meeting human needs. One such novel solution is propelling ships by *"sky sails,"* potentially saving up to 60% of fuel for 50,000 freighters at competitive costs. Another is to give surfaces the characteristics of lotus leaves so that they will become self-cleaning. The markets of the future will belong to such solutions.

The development of countries, which are as yet not industrialized, is impossible without dematerialized solutions. Entrepreneurial success on all economic levels, including exporting goods, blueprints, and services, will also depend on striving for maximum resource productivity, as will gaining independence from those possessing raw materials – including energy carriers – and preventing armed conflicts over access to natural resources.

While increasing material productivity, reducing erosion, and using land optimally are necessary for moving toward sustainability, they are not the only conditions. Welfare is more than material wealth and consumption. Welfare includes factors such as employment, adequate income, equity, education, health, safety (freedom from violence), environmental aesthetics, social security, and leisure.

Goals for sustainability and suitable indicators

Creating new values for civil society will require the casting of goals with a definite time frame. Wherever possible, these goals should be encapsulated in measurable physical terms so that development can be managed. To the extent that value creation requires natural resources, the goals have to respect the laws of nature.

Specifics, including policy instruments, for protecting nature's services may vary for differing geographic and geological conditions. However, since humankind has only one planet, the fruits of the commons and its protection must be shared fairly.

The following global goals have been suggested in the literature for the target year 2050:

–   The ecological footprint per person should not exceed 1.2 hectares.
–   The worldwide per capita consumption of nonrenewable resources should be less than five to six tons per year. (This goal implies a tremendous increase in resource efficiency in industrialized countries. In Germany, for instance, it means a Factor 10 increase, requiring a yearly absolute improvement in resource productivity of almost 5%, starting now. In the United States, the resource use would have to decline about a factor of 15, and in Finland close to a factor of 20).

These goals must be discussed further. If the dematerializations indicated above for industrialized countries were achieved, they would allow developing countries to increase their use of natural resources for improving their quality of life without jeopardizing the overall goal of global sustainability.

Because it is impossible to manage a system without metrics, we must agree on appropriate indicators. These must satisfy six criteria: 1) they must be based on measurable quantities 2) they must be generally applicable on a "cradle to grave" basis 3) they must be directionally true 4) they must be cost-efficient in their application 5) they must be based on scientific evidence and on broadly accepted guidelines such as the above definition for eco-innovation and 6) they must respect and relate to the laws of nature (for instance, economic indicators must go beyond conventional measures of gross domestic product (GDP)).

As to the ecological dimensions of sustainability, calculations of total material requirements (TMR), from cradle to grave material input per service unit (MIPS), and ecological rucksack (total material input for manufacturing a product, from cradle to the point of sale in kilograms, minus the mass of the products itself in kilograms) measurements satisfy these requirements. In addition, value per unit of weight, and labor input per unit of weight of industrial goods have been suggested as initial indicators. Furthermore, great need remains for indices that reflect the resource implications of progress in the institutional, social, and economic dimensions of sustainability.

Economic policies

No incentives or policies currently exist for a sufficiently resource-efficient economy. Adjusting the economic and fiscal framework is therefore the most fundamental and urgent prerequisite for moving toward sustainability.

For this shifting, a strong preference seems to be emerging for economic instruments, such as environmental tax reform and market-creation policies, including tradable permits. Instead of value-added taxation, for instance, it may be more efficient to tax the use of natural resources before goods for final use have been produced, while lowering taxation of labor accordingly. But because of market failures, economic instruments may not work in all cases; therefore, other instruments and measures should be considered, such as information and coordination instruments and command-and-control mechanisms, for instance adjusting norms and standards.

The choice of policy options should depend on their efficiency in dematerializing goods and services at the least possible cost to civil society.

Today, public procurement of goods and services amounts to some 15 to 20% of final consumption. Preference to dematerialized goods, infrastructures, and services could give the manufacturing sector a powerful incentive to increase resource productivity. In Germany, this may be a particularly attractive option, as it has been shown that some 20% of resource-input production costs could be saved on average without negatively affecting outputs.

Agreement has also emerged in civil society that improving education and training on all levels, as well as enhancing the public availability of relevant information, will play a central role as part of a progressive strategy.

Basics for approaching sustainability

1 The key flaw of the present mainstream economic model is its lack of incentives for increasing the productivity of natural resources.
2 This flaw creates a dangerous situation because the present rate of resource use:
   – cannot be globalized since at least two planets would be needed as a resource basis.
   – does not permit the fair development of poorer countries;
   – increases the potential for worldwide conflict.
   – increases the dependence of many countries on others that are more blessed with natural resources.

- can deplete or exhaust nature's services, without which humankind cannot survive.

3 Among the policies that governments can institute to improve the situation, preference is emerging for economic instruments, *inter alia,* aiming simultaneously at dematerialization as well as at job creation by shifting taxes and overheads from labor to natural resources.

4 During the next few decades, the productivity in using natural material resources has to be improved by at least a factor of ten compared to current resource consumption in western countries.

5 The use of fossil energy carriers must be abandoned as rapidly as possible through a switch to inexhaustible sources of energy with the help of dematerialized technology.

6 Goals for sustainable value generation, expressed in measurable terms, are required for monitoring and managing progress toward a future with a future.

7 Indicators related to resource saving have to be set for monitoring ecological, economic, social, and institutional developments.

8 As new technical and societal developments tend to require ten to twenty years to take hold, dematerialization must commence immediately.

9 A single country cannot bring about the needed changes, but Europe with its historic experiences, economic power, and technical skills has a realistic chance to lead humankind to a more promising future.

Note: The first World Resources Forum (www. worldresourcesforum.org) will be held in Davos, Switzerland, on September 16, 2009. Consult also Position Paper 01/08 at www. factor10-institute.org.

Glossary

Abiotic raw materials are all materials which are extracted directly from nature, are not renewable and not yet processed, including extracted materials which are not used (for example mining waste, excavated material from constructing a basement or a house, other excavated materials, etc.).

Air is included in the MIPS concept if it is changed in its chemical or physical characteristics.

Auxiliary materials are materials which are involved in a process but merely fulfill an auxiliary function (for example release agents).

Basic materials and *building materials* are materials or substances which are employed in a process (for example, steel, PVC or glass).

Biotic raw materials are all organic materials extracted directly from nature, for example, soilage, mushrooms, trees, fish, wild animals, unprocessed cotton.

Capacity utilization denotes the actual use of the volume or the capacity for which a good is designed (for example, a fully-occupied car, a half-filled dishwasher).

Capital in the language of economics denotes the total assets of money, machinery, facilities, as well as land. To describe monetary assets only, the term financial capital is used.

Capital productivity is the amount of goods and services produced per unit of capital employed. If the same product can be produced in the same quantity and quality on two different machines which have different prices, then capital productivity is higher if the cheaper machine is purchased.

COPS (Cost Per Unit of Service) refers to the monetary costs for a defined service (a defined unit of utility or service) which is rendered either on a person-to-person basis or by machines (for example, dispensing cash by an automated teller machine).

Cycles are natural and technical material flows which return to their original state at their point of origin. There are no technical cycles without losses.

Dematerialization is the reduction of material natural resources to satisfy human needs by technical means.

Earth-moving includes all movements of earth caused by technology in the construction, agriculture, and forestry sectors, in other words, overburdens, plowed earth, erosion, etc.

Eco-efficiency means the delivery of competitively priced goods and services which satisfy human needs and produce quality of life while progressively reducing ecological impacts and resource intensity, through the life cycle, to a level at least in line with the earth's estimated carrying capacity (following Frank Bosshardt, *Business Council for Sustainable Development*, 1991).

Eco-industry is that part of industry which conducts eco-innovation in a pro-active and verifiable manner, including businesses that provide new solutions for legal standards, norms, and requirements.

Eco-innovation means the creation of novel and competitively priced goods, processes, systems, services, and procedures that can satisfy human needs and bring quality of life to all people with a life-cycle-wide minimal use of natural resources (material including energy carriers and surface area) per unit of output, and a minimal release of toxic substances. (INNOVA EUROPE Report of the EU Commission, 2008)

Eco-intelligent (eco-efficient) service is the purpose oriented generation of utility within the technosphere by employing technical means with the highest possible resource productivity and the lowest possible emissions of harmful substances.

Ecological price encompasses the entire material input or the material added value in units of weight from the cradle of the resources to the product when it is ready to be sold and to provide a service. It is the ecological rucksack of the product plus the product's weight.

Ecological rucksack of a product is defined as its material input from the cradle to the point of sale, MI (including energy) minus its own weight (own mass). Unit: kilograms, metric tons.

Ecological rucksack of a service is the sum of the shares of the rucksacks of the technical means employed (for example, equipment, vehicles, and buildings), plus the sum of its share of materials and energy used while the technical means are employed.

Ecosphere is mankind's natural environment.

Efficiency: The effectiveness with which means are introduced into an existing process in order to attain a defined output (see, in contrast: productivity).

Emissions are contaminations of the air, noises, vibrations, light, heat, radiation, and similar energetic or material phenomena which come from a facility, a vehicle or piece of equipment.

Energy carriers are materials of all aggregate states which yield thermal energy (for example mineral oil, oil sands, coal or firewood).

Environment encompasses animals, plants, microorganisms, water, air, and soils as well as all the interactions between them.

Environmental capital is a metaphor for describing the stock of natural resources. This term is somewhat strange from a natural science point of view. Nothing can be removed from nature or even moved within nature by technology without changing its functions, and thus the life-sustaining services of nature. The market prices for abiotic and biotic raw materials, water, soil, and air do not reflect what economists call environmental "externalities," and most likely they never will, because removing resources from their natural positions inevitably causes changes of environmental services, changes that are rarely predictable with scientific methods, nor can they ever be completely measured, stimulated, qualified, quantified, or localized.

Perhaps the term "environmental capital" is useful when discussing the issue of quantities of natural resources remaining in place for future generations. But this can meaningfully be computed only in terms of kilograms or metric tons.

Environmental changes (for example, climatic change) are the consequence of human impacts on the services of nature by setting flows of natural material in motion or denaturalizing surfaces.

Environmental media are soil, water, and air.

Environmental stress potential is the capacity of a process, a good, or a service to cause changes in environmental services. It is modeled approximately by MIPS.

External environmental effects (externalities): Unintended and typically negative (cost-inducing) effects of goods, processes, systems, services, and behaviors which become effective via environmental media. Frequently, the costs of such external effects must be borne by the general public. An external effect of smoking, for example, is health problems due to second-hand smoke. An external effect of fossil fuel use is damage to historic buildings on account of air pollution.

Factor 4 is the goal of dematerializing the material design of human well-being on average by a factor of four, as an interim step on the way to sustainability.

Factor 10 is a metaphor for the strategic economic goal of approaching sustainability by increasing overall resource productivity tenfold on average in industrialized countries. It has been suggested that by 2050 the worldwide per capita consumption of non-renewable resources should not exceed five to six metric tons annually. Accordingly, Germany should dematerialize its economy by a factor of ten, whereas Japan should do so by a factor of six, the United States would need to reach a factor of fifteen, and Finland a factor of nineteen, based on present per capita consumption of natural resources. Many experts are convinced that without radical dematerialization in advanced countries, sustainability cannot be reached. *Factor X and Factor Y* are variations on Factor 10, with the purpose of indicating the unavoidable uncertainty in individual cases regarding how far dematerialization can and must go.

FIPS (in German: Flächeninput pro Einheit Service, surface area per unit of service) is a robust and directionally reliable indicator for the comparison of functionally comparable goods or services regarding their surface area requirements. A quantitative measure for the "use of natural surface area" per unit of utility or unit of service. The "ecological surface area price" for utility.

Goods are machines, products, equipment, objects, means of transport, buildings, infrastructures (including works of art and musical instruments).

Greenhouse effect: Sunlight falls on the Earth's surface, where it is transformed into warmth and partly reflected towards outer space. Some constituent parts of the Earth's atmosphere, especially water vapor and carbon dioxide, are involved in the process of capturing part of this warmth. If this natural greenhouse effect did not exist, the Earth's average temperature would not be 15 °C, but as cold as −18/19 °C. Mankind is currently changing the relative amounts of important greenhouse gases in the atmosphere, especially carbon dioxide, methane, nitrous oxide, chlorofluorocarbons, and ozone. As a result, the man-made greenhouse effect is added to the natural greenhouse effect, changing the Earth's climate.

Infrastructure denotes the basic installations or substructure on which the continuity and the growth of an economy rest, such as roads, schools, transportation and information networks.

Input includes everything which is employed in a process. In the MIPS concept, the inputs are materials (including energy).

Life cycle-wide ("from cradle to cradle") means encompassing all phases of a product's life, that is, resource extraction, production, distribution, storage, use, and recycling/disposal.

Material flows as defined in the MIPS concept are all
movements of materials in the ecosphere and the
technosphere by technical means.

Material input (MI) is the totality of natural materials that
are moved and extracted by technical means from their
natural places in order to manufacture a product or provide
a service. MI also includes all natural materials that are
needed to make the necessary energy available. MI is
measured in metric tons or kilograms.

MI factors or rucksack factors (MIF) are the material intensity
values for individual materials (raw, basic, and building
materials). Unit: kilogram per kilogram or kilogram per
megajoule etc.

MIPS = MI/S (material input per unit of service) is the life
cycle-wide input of natural material (MI) which is employed
in order to fulfill a human desire or need (S) by technical
means.

MIPS is a robust and directionally reliable indicator for directly
comparing functionally comparable goods or services
regarding their material or energy requirements. MIPS
(= MI/S) is a quantitative measure for the "use of natural
materials and energy" or the "ecological materials and
energy price" per unit of utility or per unit of service. MI
is given in kilograms (or tons); S has no dimension and
must therefore be defined stringently for each individual
case (for example "cleaning five kilograms of clothing" or
"transporting one person for a distance of one kilometer").

MIPS = material input per unit of service = ecological total
costs (referring to materials and energy use) for using a
service unit provided by a service machine = ecological
costs of use for a product = the subsidy provided by the

environment per unit of service = a measure for resource productivity of services.

Nanogram: A unit of measurement, the prefix "nano" means "one billionth."

Natural location of resources is the place where they are found in nature and from where they are technically removed.

Natural resources are all naturally available abiotic and biotic raw materials (minerals, fossil and nuclear energy carriers, plants, wild animals, and biodiversity), flow resources (wind, geothermal, tidal, and solar energy), air, water, soil, and space (land use for human settlements, infrastructures, industry, mineral extraction, agriculture, and forestry).

Operating materials are materials that serve to carry out processes, but are not present in the resulting product (for example, cleaning and cooling agents).

Output encompasses everything that results from a process, a procedure or a behavior. Output need not be material in nature; enjoyment and pleasure can also be outputs.

Person-kilometer: The number of people transported multiplied by the distance in kilometers yields the number of person-kilometers (pkm). A unit of measurement for transportation performance. Transporting one person over a distance of one kilometer means transportation performance of one person-kilometer. In this sense, the transportation performance is the same if two people are transported over a distance of one kilometer each or if one person is transported over a distance of two kilometers.

Processes are procedures or techniques in which inputs are intentionally transformed into at least *one* output (for example, shaped sheet metal, a chemical, or enjoyment of a painting).

Product: A usable result of a technical or natural process.

Serviceable products are goods that were produced for use or consumption and that can provide utility by being used (for example, robots, sundials, automobiles, mousetraps, spoons, oil paintings). In addition, there are non-serviceable goods, such as bars of gold or aluminum profiles.

Industrial products are foods, medicines, infrastructures, machines, equipment, tools, instruments, vehicles, and buildings produced with technical means in the technosphere.

Natural products are gases, liquids, or solids produced by nature when appropriate materials, energy, water, and nutrients interact.

Productivity: yield of production of goods or services. While efficiency describes the effectiveness of the use of the available means, productivity measures the result, in other words, the yield of products and services, regardless of which means were employed to obtain the result.

Productivity of labor: In this book, we use the term to denote the amount of products or services which can be produced with a given amount of work, that is, within a given period of time by a given number of people, usually by employing technology. Therefore, productivity of labor is the amount of goods or services produced per hour and per person working. Productivity can be increased by boosting *efficiency*, that is, if available means of production are exploited in an optimal fashion. But as a rule, much greater increases can be achieved by employing entirely new production methods (machines, organization of work, management).

Prosperity is not to be confused with material wealth. Prosperity also includes health, freedom from fear,

displacement, and social marginalization, as well as the
opportunity for self-determination, freedom of opinion, and
the inviolability of the dignity of the individual insofar as
one bears complete responsibility for one's own decisions.

Resource productivity is the amount of goods and services
which can be produced per unit of input of resources
(materials, surface area, energy).

Service (technically *provided service*) is the purpose-oriented
generation of utility within the technosphere by employing
technical means. All man-made services require the use of
technology. Services can be rendered either by humans or by
machines

Services of the ecosphere (services of nature) are provided
free of charge, and without exception they are necessary
for supporting life. For example, they include sufficient
availability of healthy water in liquid form and clean air
for breathing, formation and preservation of fertile soils,
protection from dangerous radiation from outer space,
diversity of species, and the reproductive power of sperms
and seeds. They cannot be produced by technical means in
any meaningful quantity, and unwise economic activities can
damage them locally as well as globally. Consequences of
damage to ecosphere services which can already be measured
today include soil erosion, extinction of species, climate
change, extreme weather conditions, scarcity of water on all
continents, and floods.

Sustainability has three fundamental dimensions: economic
social, and ecologic. The ecological dimension determines
the corridors for economic and social developments because
the availability of natural resources is limited and the vital
services of the ecosphere can be diminished or annihilated,
but not replaced, by human activity. Sustainability is the

capacity of the economic system to provide prosperity for all and, at the same time, to secure the natural, social, and economic foundations that this capacity depends on for the future. Achieving sustainability necessitates overcoming current challenges today and not shifting the burden to the shoulders of future generations.

Sustainable economic activity is service-oriented and knowledge-intensive. It creates prosperity comparable to the level attained in industrialized countries at the beginning of the 21st century with at most one-tenth the use of natural resources. Dematerialization is a necessary, but not sufficient condition for approaching sustainability.

Technosphere: The area of life created by mankind using natural resources and by technical means.

Total Material Flow (TMF) or *Total Material Requirement (TMR)* is a robust economic indicator to measure the annual total amount of natural materials (abiotic, biotic, and movements of earth)–including rucksacks–which are processed through an economic area by technical means (metric tons per year). The term MI (TMR) is also used regarding the MI of products and services when the rucksack categories abiotic, biotic, and movements of earth are presented in added form.

Utility is a measure for the capacity of goods to satisfy people's needs. MIPS is the ecological price of utility.

Wastes are materials or products rejected as useless or worthless. In many countries wastes must be recycled or disposed of in legally prescribed ways.

Metals	Specification	Material Intensity metric tons					Territory
		Abiotic Material	Biotic Material	Water	Air	Moved Soil	
Aluminum	primary	37.00	–	1047.7	10.870	–	Europe
	secondary	0.85	–	30.7	0.948	–	Europe
	wrought alloy	35.28	–	996.8	10.374	–	Europe
	cast alloy	8.11	–	234.1	2.932	–	Europe
	average	18.98	–	539.2	5.909	–	Europe
Lead	(estimated)	15.60	–	–	–	–	World
Ferrochromium	low carbon, 60% Cr	21.58	–	504.9	5.075	–	World
Ferromanganese	high carbon, 75% Cr	13.54	–	221.4	2.300	–	World
	high carbon, 75% Mn	16.69	–	193.8	2.231	–	World
Ferro molybdenum	(estimated)	748.00	–	1286.0	9.500	–	World
Ferro nickel	25% Ni	60.33	–	615.9	9.726	–	World
Gold	(estimated)	540000.00	–	–	–	–	World
Copper	50% primary, 50% secondary	179.07	–	236.39	1.160	–	World
	secondary	2.38	–	85.50	1.319	–	World
	primary	348.47	–	367.20	1.603	–	World
Nickel	–	141.29	–	233.30	40.825	–	Germany
Platinum	–	320300.00	–	193000.00	13800.000	–	World
Silver	(estimated)	7500.00	–	–	–	–	World

Metals	Specification	Material Intensity/metric tons					Territory
		Abiotic Material	Biotic Material	Water	Air	Moved Soil	
	plate, hot dipped galvanised, basic oxygen steel	9.32	–	81.9	0.772	–	World
	rebar, wire rod, engineering steel; electric arc furnace route	1.47	–	58.8	0.519	–	World
Steel	rebar, wire rod, engineering steel; blast furnace route	8.14	–	63.7	0.444	–	World
	plate, blast furnace route	8.05	–	55.7	0.436	–	World
	hot rolled, blast furnace route	7.63	–	56.0	0.414	–	World
	plate, electrogalvanized, blast furnace	9.42	–	75.4	0.650	–	World
	cold rolled, blast furnace route	8.51	–	74.8	0.492	–	World
Stainless steel	18%Cr; 9%Ni	14.43	–	205.1	2.825	–	Europe
	17%Cr; 12%Ni	17.94	–	240.3	3.382	–	Europe
Tin	import mix Germany	8486.00	–	10958.0	149.000	–	Germany
	electrolytic	22.18	–	343.7	2.282	–	Germany
Zinc	high-grade zinc, (secondary) IS	19.36	–	86.5	42.290	–	Germany
	mix	21.76	–	305.1	8.283	–	Germany

Basic Materials	Specification	Material Intensity metric tons					Territory
		Abiotic Material	Biotic Material	Water	Air	Moved Soil	
Alumina	Al_2O_3; Bayer-process	7.43	–	58.6	0.450	–	Germany
Borax	synthetic ($Na_2O2B_2O_310H_2O$)	5.75	–	13.0	0.430	–	Germany
Boric acid	$B_2O_33H_2O$	7.61	–	16.2	1.080	–	Germany
Diabase	crushed	1.42	–	6.1	0.050	–	Germany
Diabase	ground	1.65	–	10.3	0.080	–	Germany
Diamonds	(estimated)	5260000.00	–	–	–	–	South Africa
Fluorspar	CaF_2	2.93	–	7.9	0.056	–	Europe
Gypsum	ground	1.83	–	10.3	0.064	–	Germany
Graphite	–	20.06	–	306.2	5.704	–	Canada
Potassium salt	(estimated)	5.69	–	–	–	–	World
Lime	limestone / dolomite; crushed	1.44	–	5.6	0.030	–	Germany
Lime	limestone / dolomite; ground	1.66	–	9.7	0.060	–	Germany
Lime	caustic lime; crushed	3.12	–	12.8	0.102	–	Germany
Lime	caustic lime; ground	3.23	–	14.7	0.120	–	Germany
Lime	calcium hydroxide	2.46	–	11.7	0.090	–	Germany
China clay	–	3.05	–	2.5	0.077	–	Germany
Sand	quartz sand	1.42	–	1.4	0.030	–	Germany
Soda	heavy, synthetic, Na_2CO_3	4.46	–	27.7	1.020	–	Germany
Rock salt	NaCl	1.24	–	2.3	0.020	–	Germany

Energy and Fuels		Specification	Material Intensity metric tons					Territory
			Abiotic Material	Biotic Material	Water	Air	Moved Soil	
Electricity		electrical power (public network)	4.70	–	83.1	0.600	–	Germany
		electrical power (industrial power producers)	2.67	–	37.9	0.640	–	Germany
Countries		electrical power, European OECD countries	1.58	–	63.8	0.425	–	Europe
		electrical power, all OECD countries	1.55	–	66.7	0.535	–	World
Lignite		H_u; 8.8 MJ/kg	9.68	–	9.2	0.023	–	Germany
Steam		16 bar; 3.117 MJ/kg	0.39	–	1.6	0.241	–	Germany
		16 bar; 3.060 MJ/kg	0.39	–	1.6	0.236	–	Germany
Diesel oil		H_u: 42.8 MJ/kg	1.36	–	9.7	0.019	–	Germany
Natural gas		H_u: 41 MJ/kg	1.22	–	0.5	0.002	–	Germany
Crude oil		–	1.22	–	4.3	0.008	–	Germany
Heating oil		light; Hu 42, 8 MJ/kg	1.36	–	9.4	0.019	–	Germany
		heavy; Hu 40, 7 MJ/kg	1.50	–	11.4	0.033	–	Germany

Energy and Fuels	Specification	Material Intensitymetric tons					Territory
		Abiotic Material	Biotic Material	Water	Air	Moved Soil	
	H$_u$: 29.4 MJ/kg	2.36	–	9.1	0.048	–	Germany
	German import mix; H$_u$: 27.5 MJ/kg	2.11	–	9.1	0.500	–	Germany
	H$_u$: 26.37 MJ/kg	17.15	–	3.7	0.016	–	Australia
	H$_u$: 27 MJ/kg	1.47	–	6.7	0.029	–	Germany
	H$_u$: 23.25 MJ/kg	5.06	–	4.6	0.017	–	World
	H$_u$: 24.9 MJ/kg	7.70	–	1.9	0.012	–	South Africa
Hard coal	H$_u$: 25.2 MJ/kg	6.11	–	3.1	0.017	–	USA
	H$_u$: 21.1 MJ/kg	1.64	–	3.9	0.008	–	China
	H$_u$: 23.44 MJ/kg	7.40	–	10.0	0.054	–	Russia
	H$_u$: 24.9 MJ/kg	2.15	–	12.9	0.036	–	Poland
	H$_u$: 20 MJ/kg	1.75	–	9.6	0.028	–	Ukraine
	H$_u$: 27.83 MJ/kg	15.32	–	3.3	0.016	–	Canada
	H$_u$: 24.1 MJ/kg	5.97	–	5.3	0.020	–	UK
	H$_u$: 20.8 MJ/kg	4.90	–	4.3	0.021	–	India

Combustion Air	Material	Specification	Airmetric tons
	Diesel oil	H_u: 42.8 MJ/kg	3.2
	Natural gas	H_u: 41 MJ/kg	3.6
	Heating oil; light	H_u: 42.8 MJ/kg	3.2
	Heating oil; heavy	H_u 40.7 MJ/kg	3.0
	Gasoline	H_u: MJ/kg	3.2
	Lignite	H_o: 8.8 MJ/kg	0.7
		H_o: 29.4 MJ/kg	2.3
		H_o: 27.5 MJ/kg	2.2
Combustion air: All specifications are entered without combustion air. When combustibles are burned, additional air (oxygen) is transformed. The amount of air needed for the burning process is listed in the adjoining column.		H_o: 26.37 MJ/kg	2.1
		H_o: 27 MJ/kg	2.1
		H_o: 23.25 MJ/kg	1.8
		H_u: 24.9 MJ/kg	2.0
	Hard coal	H_o: 25.2 MJ/kg	2.0
		Hu: 21.1 MJ/kg	1.7
		H_o: 23.44 MJ/kg	1.8
		H_u: 24.9 MJ/kg	2.0
		H_u: 20 MJ/kg	1.6
		H_u 27.83 MJ/kg	2.2
		H_u 24.1 MJ/kg	1.9
		H_o: 20.8 MJ/kg	1.6

Chemicals	Specification	Material Intensity metric tons					Territory
		Abiotic Material	Biotic Material	Water	Air	Moved Soil	
Acetone	–	3.19	–	18.7	1.890	–	Germany
Acrylnitril	–	2.56	–	93.2	5.047	–	Europe
Allyl chloride	–	6.93	–	140.7	2.441	–	Europe
Aluminum chloride	–	8.61	–	110.6	1.150	–	Germany
Ammonia	–	1.85	–	10.1	5.044	–	Europe
Liquid ammonium nitrate urea (LAU)	fertilizer	1.43	–	58.0	0.990	–	Germany
Aniline, aminobenzen	C_6H_7N	8.21	–	148.8	3.829	–	Germany
Benzene	C_6H_6	4.32	–	28.2	2.190	–	Germany
Bisphenol-A	–	5.00	–	88.5	2.519	–	Europe
Chlorine	–	3.84	–	100.9	1.091	–	Europe
Diammonium phosphate	fertilizer	7.07	–	50.8	3.570	–	Germany
Dimethylformamide	–	1.53	–	5.3	3.722	–	Europe
Diphenylmethane diisocyanate	–	5.20	–	440.8	3.892	–	Europe
Epichlorhydrin C_3H_5ClO	–	15.42	–	319.5	5.685	–	Europe
Ethylene benzol	–	4.45	–	30.5	2.186	–	Europe
Ethylene	–	3.89	–	25.8	1.960	–	Germany
Ethylene glycol	–	2.90	–	133.5	2.293	–	Europe
Formaldehyde, methanal	–	1.11	–	30.0	0.980	–	Germany
Fumaric acid	from maleic acid	7.28	–	313.7	0.750	–	Europe
	from maleic acid anhydrite	3.23	–	140.1	0.904	–	Europe
Urea	–	3.45	–	44.6	1.820	–	Germany
Isobutyraldehdes	–	2.21	–	7.9	1.073	–	Europe

Chemicals	Specification	Material Intensity metric tons						Territory
		Abiotic Material	Biotic Material	Water	Air	Moved Soil		
Potassic fertilizer	60% K₂O	11.32	–	10.6	0.070	–		Germany
Calcium ammonium nitrate	fertilizer (mixture of CACO₃ and NH₄NO₃)	5.48	–	39.3	2.190	–		Germany
Maleic acid	from exhaust gas of phthalic anhydride production	5.01	–	216.7	3.543	–		Europe
Maleic acid anhydrite	–	2.80	–	118.3	0.589	–		Europe
Methane	–	1.38	–	2.0	3.903	–		Europe
Methanol	–	1.67	–	4.5	3.873	–		Europe
(mono)ammonium phosphate	fertilizer	7.36	–	50.6	3.680	–		Germany
Sodium hydroxide	NaOH	2.76	–	90.3	1.064	–		Europe
Naphtha	–	1.69	–	13.9	0.047	–		Germany
Neopentylglycol	–	1.81	–	15.8	0.958	–		Europe
Nitrobenzene	–	4.95	–	93.1	2.698	–		Germany
Pentane	–	1.98	–	109.7	2.148	–		Europe
Phenol	–	3.19	–	18.7	1.890	–		Germany
Phosgene	–	4.95	–	125.3	0.608	–		Germany
Poyacrylonitrile	–	14.22	–	351.2	10.516	–		Europe
Polyether polyole	–	8.27	–	465.9	3.515	–		Europe
Polymethylene di(phenylisocyanate)	–	9.53	–	167.4	2.902	–		Germany
Propylene oxide	–	4.61	–	24.2	3.322	–		Germany
Propylene	–	1.74	–	87.5	1.495	–		Europe

Chemicals	Specification	Material Intensity metric tons					Territory
		Abiotic Material	Biotic Material	Water	Air	Moved Soil	
P-xylole	–	5.82	–	50.8	2.936	–	Europe
Soot	–	2.58	–	7.1	2.538	–	UK
Hydrochloric acid	solution 37%	3.03	–	40.7	0.380	–	Germany
Oxygen	liquid	4.66	–	1084.6	2.500	–	Germany
	gas	2.58	–	137.0	1.704	–	Europe
Sulfuric acid	H_2SO_4	0.25	–	4.1	0.700	–	Germany
Sorbitol	–	1.10	–	22.8	1.607	–	Germany
Starch	–	1.07	–	22.1	1.560	–	Germany
Nitrogen	liquid	0.81	–	33.2	1.221	–	Europe
	gas	0.19	–	7.7	1.051	–	Europe
Styrene	–	5.91	–	42.0	2.864	–	Germany
Terephthalic acid	–	4.85	–	141.7	2.578	–	Europe
Toluole diisocyanate	–	8.56	–	490.6	4.092	–	Europe
Triple superphosphate	fertilizer	3.44	–	23.3	1.290	–	Germany
Water glass	solution 35%	1.18	–	6.3	0.292	–	Germany
Hydrogen	chlorine–alkali–electrolysis	2.52	–	93.7	0.704	–	Europe

Plastics	Specification	Material Intensity metric tons					Territory
		Abiotic Material	Biotic Material	Water	Air	Moved Soil	
ABS	–	3.97	–	206.9	3.751	–	Europe
Epoxy resin	–	13.73	–	289.9	5.501	–	Europe
Polystyrene	general purpose; GPPS	2.51	–	164.0	2.802	–	Europe
	EPS granulate	2.50	–	137.7	2.475	–	Europe
	high impact; hips	2.78	–	175.3	3.150	–	Europe
Polyamide / P.A. 6.6	–	5.51	–	921.0	4.613	–	Europe
Polycarbonate	–	6.94	–	212.2	4.700	–	Europe
	foil	3.01	–	167.6	1.840	–	Europe
Polyethylene	high density HD	2.52	–	105.9	1.904	–	Europe
	low density LD	2.49	–	122.2	1.617	–	Europe
	linear low density LLD	2.12	–	162.1	2.805	–	Europe
Polyethylene terephtalat	yarn	6.45	–	294.2	3.723	–	Europe
		8.10	–	278.0	3.730	–	World
Polyester	resin, gelcoat external application	5.11	–	188.0	2.895	–	Europe
	resin, gelcoat internal application	4.32	–	167.0	2.434	–	Europe
	resin, ISO NPG	5.40	–	208.7	3.209	–	Europe
	resin, OS	5.62	–	235.4	3.459	–	Europe
Polypropylene	granulate	2.09	–	35.8	1.482	–	Europe
	injection moulding	4.24	–	205.5	3.373	–	Europe
Polytetrafluorethylene	–	18.81	–	456.9	6.373	–	Europe
Polyurethane	rigid foam	6.31	–	505.1	3.563	–	Europe
	flexible foam	7.52	–	532.4	3.420	–	Europe

Plastics	Specification	Material Intensity metric tons					Territory
		Abiotic Material	Biotic Material	Water	Air	Moved Soil	
Polyvinyl chloride	foam	17.34	–	679.4	11.573	–	Europe
	bulk	3.47	–	305.3	1.703	–	Europe
	emulsified	3.65	–	197.5	2.463	–	Europe
	suspended	3.33	–	176.6	1.693	–	Europe
Styrol buradien rubber; SBR	–	5.70	–	146.0	1.650	–	Germany

Construction Materials	Specification	Material Intensity metric tons					Territory
		Abiotic Material	Biotic Material	Water	Air	Moved Soil	
Concrete	–	1.33	–	3.4	0.044	–	Germany
Cellulose flake	–	1.71	–	6.7	0.270	–	Germany
Roofing tile	–	2.11	–	5.3	0.065	–	Germany
Cement	Portland cement	3.22	–	16.9	0.332	–	Germany
Cement	Portland blast-furnace cement	2.79	–	18.8	0.298	–	Germany
Cement	blast-furnace cement	2.22	–	21.3	0.254	–	Germany
Sheet glass	float glass	2.95	–	11.6	0.743	–	Germany
Man-made mineral fibres	glass wool	4.66	–	46.0	1.800	–	Germany
Man-made mineral fibres	rock wool	4.00	–	39.7	1.690	–	Germany
Granite	slabs, ground, polished	1.92	–	3.4	0.593	–	Germany
Sand-lime brick	–	1.28	–	2.0	0.013	–	Germany
Stoneware pipe	–	2.88	–	32.9	0.240	–	Germany
Perlite	(estimated)	2.04	–	6.8	0.043	–	Germany
Cellular concrete	400 kg/m³	2.51	–	15.0	0.263	–	Germany
Cellular concrete	500 kg/m³	2.28	–	13.4	0.219	–	Germany
Cellular concrete	500 kg/m³ statically reinforced	2.64	–	14.6	0.278	–	Germany
Cellular concrete	600 kg/m³	2.10	–	11.5	0.169	–	Germany
Cellular concrete	600 kg/m³ statically reinforced	2.37	–	12.1	0.230	–	Germany
Foam glass	–	6.71	–	152.6	2.799	–	Europe
Brick	lightweight clay brick (PS)/solid clay brick	2.11	–	5.7	0.047	–	Germany
Brick	lightweight clay brick (saw dust)	1.97	–	5.4	0.038	–	Germany

Others	Specification	Material Intensity metric tons					Territory
		Abiotic Material	Biotic Material	Water	Air	Moved Soil	
Aramid fibre	–	37.03	–	940.4	19.574	–	Europe
Cotton	USA west	8.60	2.90	6814.0	2.740	5.01	USA
Container glass	primary; special applications	3.04	–	17.1	0.716	0.14	Germany
	53% cullet	1.72	–	13.4	0.576	0.06	Germany
	88% cullet	0.87	–	10.9	0.479	0.01	Germany
	chipboard	0.68	0.65	18.4	0.292	–	Germany
	plywood	2.00	9.13	23.6	0.541	–	Germany
Wood	Douglas fir wood (baked; cut timber)	0.63	4.37	9.2	0.166	–	Germany
	Spruce wood (baked; cut timber)	0.68	4.72	9.4	0.156	–	Germany
	hardboard/ molded fiberboard	2.91	–	49.1	0.980	–	Germany
	Pine wood (baked, cut timber)	0.86	5.51	10.0	0.129	–	Germany
	fiberboard (average density)	1.96	–	32.9	0.481	–	Germany
Fibre glass	E-glass	6.22	–	94.5	2.088	–	Europe
	R-glass	10.84	–	296.3	2.007	–	Europe
Carbon fibre	PAN	58.09	–	1794.9	38.000	–	Europe
		61.12	–	2411.5	33.387	–	Europe
Leather	chrome tanned	12.30	–	515.0	2.800	–	Europe
	vegetable tanned leather	9.20	12.60	446.0	2.400	–	Europe
	vegetable tanned weight leather	3.30	12.60	176.0	0.900	–	Europe
Linoleum	–	2.01	0.35	6.7	1.992	–	Germany

Others	Specification	Material Intensity metric tons					Territory
		Abiotic Material	Biotic Material	Water	Air	Mowed Soil	
	bleached	9.17	2.56	303.0	1.275	–	Europe
	not bleached	8.94	2.38	268.1	1.289	–	Europe
	chipboard	0.30	0.22	24.9	0.070	–	Europe
	corrugated cardboard	1.86	0.75	93.6	0.325	–	Europe
	primary newsprint	0.38	0.94	3.5	0.078	–	Europe
Paper and board	secondary newsprint	0.24	0.04	14.8	0.050	–	Europe
	sulphate pulp (bleached)	2.61	2.64	112.1	0.413	–	Europe
	sulphate pulp (unbleached)	3.09	2.42	93.3	0.521	–	Europe
	sulphite pulp (bleached)	4.38	2.64	185.2	0.655	–	Europe
	sulphite pulp (unbleached)	2.59	2.42	141.9	0.413	–	Europe

Transport	Specification	Material Intensity g/tkm (only transport)					Territory
		Abiotic Material	Biotic Material	Water	Air	Moved Soil	
Seagoing vessels	all	6.00	–	52.0	10.000	–	Germany
	tanker	4.00	–	31.0	5.000	–	Germany
	container vessel	9.00	–	80.0	17.000	–	Germany
	cargo boat	10.00	–	90.0	19.000	–	Germany
Canal boats	all	24.00	–	160.0	35.000	–	Germany
	vessel	25.00	–	163.0	37.000	–	Germany
	push boat	20.00	–	130.0	29.000	–	Germany
	four lighter barge train	19.00	–	130.0	20.000	–	Germany
Cargo trains	all German trains	77.00	–	3568.0	34.000	–	Germany
	diesel traction	55.00	–	149.0	56.000	–	Germany
	electric traction	83.00	–	4365.0	29.000	–	Germany
	all	218.00	–	1910.0	209.000	–	Germany
	truck, < 2.8 metric tons	1336.00	–	11630.0	1331.000	–	Germany
Truck transport of cargo	all trucks 2.8 metric tons	450.00	–	4124.0	144.000	–	Germany
	tractor-trailer, 8 metric tons	107.00	–	927.0	102.000	–	Germany
	tractor-trailer	89.00	–	731.0	100.000	–	Germany

Water	Specification	Material Intensity g/tkm (only transport)					Territory
		Abiotic Material	Biotic Material	Water	Air	Moved Soil	
Drinking water	–	0.01	–	1.3	0.001	–	Germany
Deonized water	(estimated)	0.08	–	2.2	0.008	–	Germany

References

Chapter 1

Brown, Lester R. 2005. *Outgrowing the Earth*. London: Earthscan Publications.

Carson, Rachel. 1962. *Silent Spring*. Boston, MA: Houghton Mifflin.

Fussler, Claude. 1997. *Driving Eco-Innovation*. Financial Times/Prentice Hall.

Hawken, Paul, et al. 2000. *Natural Capitalism*. Back Bay Books.

Lehmann, Harry and Thorsten Reetz. 1995. *Zukunftsenergien*. Stuttgart: Hirzel.

Liedtke, Christa and T. Busch (eds.). 2005. *Materialeffizienz*. Munich: Ökom Verlag.

Meadows, Danella et al. 2004. *Limits to Growth – The 30 Year Update*, White River Junction, VT: Chelsea Green.

Mitsuhashi, Tadahiro. 2003. *Japan's Green Comeback*, Pelanduk Pubns Sdn Bhd.

Rocholl, M. et al. 2006. *Factor X and the EU – How to make Europe the most resource and energy efficient economy in the World*, Aachener Stiftung Kathy Beys, www. aachenfoundation.org.

Sachs, Wolfgang, et al. 2005 *Fair Future. Begrenzte Ressourcen
    und Globale Gerechtigkeit. Ein Report des Wuppertal
    Instituts*, Munich: C. H. Beck.

Schmidt-Bleek, Friedrich: *Gedanken zum Ökologischen
    Strukturwandel*, Positionspapier, Wuppertal Institut,
    1992. Later published in: *Regulatory, Toxicology and
    Pharmacology*, 18: 3., Academic Press Inc., December 1993.

Schmidt-Bleek, Friedrich. 1994. *Wie viel Umwelt braucht der
    Mensch? – MIPS, das Maß für ökologisches Wirtschaften*,
    Birkhäuser Verlag.

Schmidt-Bleek, Friedrich. 2000. *Das MIPS-Konzept – Faktor 10*,
    Munich: Knaur.

Stahel, Walter, et al. 1997. *Ökointelligente Produkte,
    Dienstleistungen und Arbeit*, Birkhäuser Verlag.

*Statement to Governments and Industry leaders by the
    International Factor 10 Club*, 1997, www.factor10-institute.
    org.

Weizsaecker E. U. von et al. 1997. *Factor 4: Doubling Wealth,
    Halving Resource Use – A Report to the Club of Rome*,
    London: Earthscan.

Chapter 2

*New Information on how Finland's Traffic System Consumes
    Natural Resources*, Report by the Finnish Minister
    for Environment and Transportation on the Resource
    Consumption of Finland's Transportation System,
    computed applying MIPS, Helsinki, April 2006, www.
    ymparisto.fi/julkaisut. Contact: Sauli Rouhinen, General
    Secretary of the Finnish Commission for Sustainability,
    sauli.rouhinen@ymparisto.fi.

Ritthoff, Michael et. al. 2002. *MIPS berechnen –*
   Ressourcenproduktivität von Produkten und
   Dienstleistungen, Wuppertal Institut. www.wupperinstitute/
   MIPS-online.de.
Schmidt-Bleek, Friedrich et al. 1998. *MAIA, Einführung in die*
   Material Input Analyse nach dem MIPS-Konzept, Wuppertal
   Texte, Birkhäuser Verlag.
Schmidt-Bleek, Friedrich et al. 1999. *Ökodesign – Vom Produkt*
   zur Dienstleistungserfüllungsmaschine, Wirtschaftskammer
   Österreich, WIFI 303, Vienna.
Schmidt-Bleek, Friedrich (ed.). 2004. *Der Ökologische*
   Rucksack – Wirtschaften für eine Zukunft mit Zukunft,
   Stuttgart: Hirzel.
Wackernagel, Mathis and William Rees. 1995. *Our Ecological*
   Footprint, Gabriola Island, BC, Canada: New Society
   Publishers.

Chapter 3

Reports about awarding of the Efficiency Price, NRW Efficiency
   Agency: NRW: www.efanrw.de.
Berichte über den R. I. O. Innovationspreis, Aachener Stiftung
   Kathy Beys: www.aachener-stiftung.de.
Ritthoff, Michael et al. 2002. *MIPS berechnen –*
   Ressourcenproduktivität von Produkten und
   Dienstleistungen, Wuppertal: Wuppertal Institut.
Schmidt-Bleek, Friedrich and C. Manstein. 1999. *Klagenfurt*
   Innovation.
www.mips-online.de, www.wupperinst.org, www.factor-x.info.
   de.

Chapter 4

Adriaanse, A. et al. 1998. *Die Materielle Basis von Industriegesellschaften*, Birkhäuser Verlag.

Boege, Stefanie. 1993. *Road Transport of Goods and the Effects on the Spatial Environment*, Wuppertal Institut.

Bringezu, Stefan. 2000. *Ressourcennutzung in Wirtschaftsräumen. Stoffstromanalysen für eine nachhaltige Raumentwicklung*, Berlin: Springer.

Bringezu, Stefan. 2004. *Erdlandung*, Stuttgart: Hirzel.

Meyers, N. and Jennifer Kent. 2001. *Perverse Subsidies*, Washington, DC: Island Press.

Schmidt-Bleek, Friedrich (ed.). 2004. *Der Ökologische Rucksack*, Stuttgart: Hirzel.

World Resources Institute. 1997. *Material Flows*, Washington, DC: World Resources Institute.

World Resources Institute. 2001. *The Weight of Nations*, Washington, DC: World Resources Institute.

Chapter 5

Brown, Lester R.. 2003. *Eco-Economy*, London: Earthscan Publications.

Global 100 Eco-Tech Awards, Japan Association for the 2005 World Exposition, 1533–1 Ibaradabasama, Nagakute-cho, Aichi 480–1101, Japan (Descriptions of environmental technologies, 160 pages).

Latif, Mojib. 2009. *Climate Change: The Point of No Return.* London: Haus Publishing.

Mooss, Heinz: Ökointelligent. *Geniale Ideen und Produkte aus Oesterreich*, Vienna: Ueberreuter 2005.

Chapter 6

Faktor Y, Magazin für Nachhaltiges Wirtschaften
Internationales Forum für Gestaltung. 1998. *Gestaltung des*
  Unsichtbaren, Berlin: Anabis Verlag.
Klemmer, Paul and Fritz Hinterberger. 1999. *Ökoeffiziente*
  Dienstleistungen, Birkhäuser Verlag.
Schmidt-Bleek, Friedrich and Ursula Tischner. 1995.
  Produktentwicklung – Nutzen gestalten – Natur schonen,
  Wirtschaftskammer Österreich, WIFI 270, Vienna.

Chapter 7

Bericht des Zukunftsrates NRW 2004: www.agenda21.nrw.de
Bierter, Willy. 1995. *Wege zum ökologischen Wohlstand*,
  Birkhäuser Verlag.
Dieren, W. van (ed.). 1995. *Taking Nature into Account*, Berlin:
  Springer.
Dosch, K.: *Ressourcenproduktivität als Chance – Ein*
  langfristiges Konjunkturprogramm für Deutschland, 2005,
  in: www.aachener-stiftung.de.
Fischer, Hartmut et al. *Wachstum und Beschäftigungsimpulse*
  rentabler Materialeinsparungen, in: Wirtschaftsdienst, Issue
  4, April 2004.
Hinterberger, Fritz et al. 1996. *Ökologische Wirtschaftspolitik*,
  Birkhäuser Verlag.
Holliday, Chad et al. 2001. *Sustainabilidy through the Market*,
  in: World Business Council for Sustainable Development.
Myers, Norman and Jennifer Kent. 2001. *Perverse Subsidies*,
  Washington, DC: Island Press.

Spangenberg, Joachim H. (ed). 2003. *Vision 2020: Arbeit, Umwelt, Gerechtigkeit – Strategien für ein zukunftsfähiges Deutschland*, Munich: Ökom.

Spangenberg, Joachim H. and S. Giljum (eds.). Special edition "Governance for Sustainable Development", *International Journal of Sustainable Development*, 8, 2005.

Stahel, Walter R.: 2006. *The Performance Economy*, Basingstoke: Palgrave, Macmillan.

Wohlmeyer, Heinrich. 2006. *Globales Schafe Scheren – Gegen die Politik des Niedergangs*, : Edition Vabcne.

Credits

All diagrams: Peter Palm, Berlin. Fig. 1 adapted from: Sachs, W.: *Fair Future*, fig. 3, p. 36; table 1 adapted from: Sachs, W. ibid., p. 35; fig. 2 adapted from: Schmidt-Bleek, F.: *Wieviel Umwelt braucht der Mensch?*, fig. 6, p. 26; fig. 3 adapted from: Bringezu, S.: *Ressourcennutzung in Wirtschaftsräumen*, fig. 5, p. 72; fig. 5 adapted from: Schmidt-Bleek, F.: see above, fig. 5, p. 25; fig. 6 adapted from: Schmidt-Bleek, F.: see above, fig. 23, p. 130; fig. 7 adapted from: Sachs, W.: see above, fig. 9, p. 70; fig. 8 adapted from: Schmidt-Bleek, F.: see above, fig. 21, p. 125; fig. 9 adapted from: Schmidt-Bleek, F.: *Das MIPS- Konzept*, p. 53; fig. 10 adapted from: Bringezu, S.: *Erdlandung*, fig. 1, p. 49; fig. 11 adapted from: Bringezu, S.: *Ressourcennutzung in Wirtschaftsräumen*, fig. 10, p. 98; fig. 12 adapted from: Schmidt-Bleek, F.: *Das MIPS-Konzept*, fig. 26, p. 234, data from R. Behrensmeier and S. Bringezu, *Wuppertal Papers* Nr. 24, Wuppertal 1995; fig. 13 adapted from: Bringezu, *Erdlandung*, fig. 7, p. 94; table 4 adapted from: ibid., table 4, p. 88; table 5 adapted from: ibid., table 3, p. 82; table 6 adapted from: John R. McNeill, *Blue Planet*, Frankfurt, New

York 2000, tablw 5.1; fig. 16 adapted from: Wuppertal Institut Jahrbuch 2004/2005, p. 109; fig. 17 adapted from: Schmidt-Bleek, F.: *Das MIPS Konzept* (see above), fig. 23, p. 203; fig. 18 adapted from: Europäisches Amt für Statistik, *Trend Chart Innovation Policy in Europe*, p. 2 and *Intellectual Property Rights in Focus* 2006.